C000241220

IMAGES OF
SPORT

GRAVESEND & NORTHFLEET FC

FORMATIVE YEARS

GRAVESEND UNITED

1893 – Club formed by merger of Gravesend FC and Gravesend Ormonde

KENT LEAGUE – Division 1

	P.	W.	D.	L.	F.	A.	Pts	Pos.
1893-94	16	6	5	5	54	33	17	4th
1894-95	22	10	4	8	36	45	20	7th
1895-96	19	1	2	16	23	81	4	11th

SOUTHERN LEAGUE – Division 1

	P.	W.	D.	L.	F.	A.	Pts	Pos.
1896-97	20	9	4	7	35	34	22	5th
1897-98	22	7	6	9	28	39	20	8th
1898-99	24	7	5	12	42	52	19	11th
1899-00	28	10	4	14	38	58	24	12th
1900-01	28	6	7	15	32	85	19	13th

Rejoined KENT LEAGUE for one season before playing succession of local friendlies

KENT LEAGUE – Division 1

	P.	W.	D.	L.	F.	A.	Pts	Pos.
1905-06	14	10	1	3	44	21	21	2nd
1906-07	14	7	1	6	42	24	15	3rd
1907-08	14	5	1	8	21	26	11	7th
1908-09	16	11	3	2	40	16	25	2nd
1909-10	22	9	5	8	34	36	23	6th
1910-11	26	8	6	12	37	53	22	7th
1911-12	28	12	5	11	64	50	29	5th
1912-13	28	7	7	14	34	52	21	12th
1913-14	30	10	6	14	50	57	26	11th

Suspended due to war – did not reform until 1932 after losing their ground

KENT AMATEUR LEAGUE – Division 1

	P.	W.	D.	L.	F.	A.	Pts	Pos.
1932-33	14	8	2	4	38	26	18	2nd

KENT LEAGUE – Division 2

	P.	W.	D.	L.	F.	A.	Pts	Pos.
1933-34	24	13	4	7	75	46	30	4th
1934-35	24	8	1	15	46	100	17	10th

KENT AMATEUR LEAGUE – Western Section

	P.	W.	D.	L.	F.	A.	Pts	Pos.
1935-36	20	16	3	1	86	32	35	1st
1936-37	20	10	3	7	41	38	23	5th
1937-38	20	12	4	4	46	24	28	3rd
1938-39	24	6	6	12	53	92	18	8th

Suspended due to war

KENT LEAGUE

	P.	W.	D.	L.	F.	A.	Pts	Pos.
1944-45	18	7	3	8	28	37	17	7th
1945-46	20	9	3	8	42	23	21	3rd

NORTHFLEET UNITED

1890 – Club formed

	P.	W.	D.	L.	F.	A.	Pts	Pos.

KENT LEAGUE – Division 1

	P.	W.	D.	L.	F.	A.	Pts	Pos.
1895-96	22	16	2	4	85	31	34	1st

SOUTHERN LEAGUE – Division 1

	P.	W.	D.	L.	F.	A.	Pts	Pos.
1896-97	20	5	4	11	24	46	14	9th
1897-98	22	4	3	15	29	60	11	11th

Rejoined KENT LEAGUE but withdrew after 7 matches –

	P.	W.	D.	L.	F.	A.	Pts	Pos.
	7	3	2	2	26	19	8	8th

WEST KENT LEAGUE

	P.	W.	D.	L.	F.	A.	Pts	Pos.
1903-04	12	1	3	8	10	31	5	7th
1904-05	20	7	3	10	37	50	17	8th
1905-06	16	7	2	7	23	26	16	5th

KENT LEAGUE – Division 1

	P.	W.	D.	L.	F.	A.	Pts	Pos.
1906-07	14	10	0	4	39	17	20	2nd
1907-08	16	14	1	1	54	13	29	1st
1908-09	16	13	1	2	51	23	27	1st
1909-10	22	17	2	3	74	31	36	1st
1910-11	26	7	4	15	38	64	18	13th
1911-12	28	10	5	13	47	48	25	8th
1912-13	28	14	5	9	58	55	33	4th
1913-14	30	17	5	8	63	49	37	4th

Suspended due to war

	P.	W.	D.	L.	F.	A.	Pts	Pos.
1919-20	24	19	3	2	70	22	41	1st
1920-21	32	21	3	8	76	40	45	3rd
1921-22	28	18	6	4	78	36	42	2nd
1922-23	32	17	5	10	88	41	39	4th
1923-24	30	15	5	10	61	35	35	4th
1924-25	34	29	1	4	114	25	59	2nd
1925-26	36	29	3	4	172	48	61	1st
1926-27	26	15	3	8	79	51	33	5th

SOUTHERN LEAGUE – Eastern Section

	P.	W.	D.	L.	F.	A.	Pts	Pos.
1927-28	34	17	7	10	83	54	41	3rd
1928-29	36	17	4	15	87	65	38	9th
1929-30	32	6	7	19	53	77	19	16th

KENT LEAGUE – Division 1

	P.	W.	D.	L.	F.	A.	Pts	Pos.
1930-31	36	21	3	12	124	59	45	5th
1931-32	36	32	2	2	138	22	66	1st
1932-33	34	28	1	5	126	50	57	2nd
1933-34	36	23	2	11	122	47	48	4th
1934-35	36	26	7	3	110	30	59	1st
1935-36	36	26	5	5	158	41	57	1st
1936-37	32	25	2	5	128	29	52	1st
1937-38	32	23	5	4	116	29	51	3rd
1938-39	28	20	4	4	125	38	44	1st

Suspended due to war – did not reform

GRAVESEND & NORTHFLEET

STADIA

IMAGES OF
SPORT

GRAVESEND & NORTHFLEET FC

PAUL HARRISON

STADIA

First published 2006

STADIA is an imprint of
Tempus Publishing Limited
The Mill, Brimscombe Port,
Stroud, Gloucestershire, GL5 2QG
www.tempus-publishing.com

© Paul Harrison, 2006

The right of Paul Harrison to be identified as the Author
of this work has been asserted in accordance with the
Copyrights, Designs and Patents Act 1988.

All rights reserved. No part of this book may be reprinted
or reproduced or utilised in any form or by any electronic,
mechanical or other means, now known or hereafter invented,
including photocopying and recording, or in any information
storage or retrieval system, without the permission in writing
from the Publishers.

British Library Cataloguing in Publication Data.
A catalogue record for this book is available from the British Library.

ISBN 0 7524 3795 X

Typesetting and origination by Tempus Publishing Limited.
Printed in Great Britain.

Contents

About the Author

Paul Harrison was born in Gravesend in 1948 and has lived in the town all his life. Educated at Dover Road Primary and Northfleet Secondary Schools, he began following Gravesend & Northfleet in 1955 as a seven-year-old in the company of his father and completed fifty years of watching the club when attending a dismal 3-0 FA Cup defeat at Kettering in 2005. These days he is only an occasional visitor to Stonebridge Road after being involved for many years as programme editor (1982-1990) and a supporters' association committeeman holding several positions of office between 1981 and 2000, at which point he relinquished all roles at the club apart from the occasional programme article. However, by a strange coincidence, another Paul Harrison then came on the scene to edit the programme and take over the website – he is no connection to the original!

This is Paul's fifth book, following *Southern League Post War Years* (1987); *Southern League First Fifty Years* (1990); *Cup Glory* (1995) and *Gravesend & Northfleet Golden Jubilee Book* in conjunction with Paul Saxby and Lionel Ball Junior. He is also proud of a unique hat-trick he achieved for two seasons in the late 1980s when he was away coach driver, programme editor and turnstile operator.

The author with grandchildren James and Amy in March 2006.

Introduction

The future looks rosy for Gravesend and Northfleet football club in their Diamond Jubilee year of 2006. Placed perfectly in the huge Thames Gateway development, their catchment area is expected to quadruple over the next ten to twenty years and, with the prospect of a new ground to go with the new training facilities and sports complex acquired last year in a deal with the local council, prospects have never been so high. For the first time since 1962 they also have a group of full-time professionals to take them on to the next step – promotion to Football League status. That status may well have been achieved many years ago had the two original local clubs, Gravesend United and Northfleet United, combined instead of staying separate despite overtures from each to the other at various times through the years.

It is often forgotten that in the late Victorian period both sides rubbed shoulders with clubs like Tottenham Hotspur, Southampton and West Ham United in the Southern League. By 1901 Tottenham had achieved the remarkable feat of winning the FA Cup as a non-League side but they were beaten 2-1 by Gravesend in a Southern League game that season – taking that to its full extreme, the present club should be in the Premiership and beating this season's FA Cup winners in a League match!

Gradually, Gravesend declined and when they lost their Pelham Road ground the club went into mothballs, never playing a match between 1914 and 1932, and Northfleet United then dominated the inter-war years. This domination became even more pronounced after an arrangement made with Tottenham in 1923 allowed the Fleet to nurture some of Spurs' brightest prospects in the school of hard knocks otherwise known as the Kent League (then a powerful league). The silverware just kept on coming, including an amazing run of five successive Kent Senior Cups in the 1920s, when it was a highly prized trophy. Each season, almost by magic, the formula was the same: progress through to the Easter Monday final and a trip to Maidstone for two, sometimes three, trainloads of supporters; the taste of victory against whoever faced them and then back to Northfleet station with the silverware and a celebration trip behind the Northfleet Silver Band along Northfleet High Street, either in an open-topped bus or on a flatbed lorry, waving to the supporters and displaying the cup to fans – before returning to the Factory Club (Blue Circle Club) for a few shandies!

The Second World War brought all this to an end and at last both clubs realised for differing reasons that it really was time to pool resources and begin a new era with a new team – Gravesend & Northfleet. That club, like so many others, has had its good and bad times in roughly equal amounts. This book is not a concise history – that was done in our Golden Jubilee book of 1996 – instead it tends to bring back memories of players and matches through images from both the distant and the recent past.

Paul Harrison
March 2006

Acknowledgements

While most of this work comes from my own collection it would have been impossible to produce the book without the help of the following people: Richard Ralph allowed me use of some of his collection of photographs; Keith Chase, David Hills and the *Kentish Times*, with special thanks to Simon Hildrew, allowed me use of their excellent action shots; Colorsport and Aerofilms have provided additional photography and John Jones and Andy Porter were a great help on the Northfleet United and Gravesend United sections.

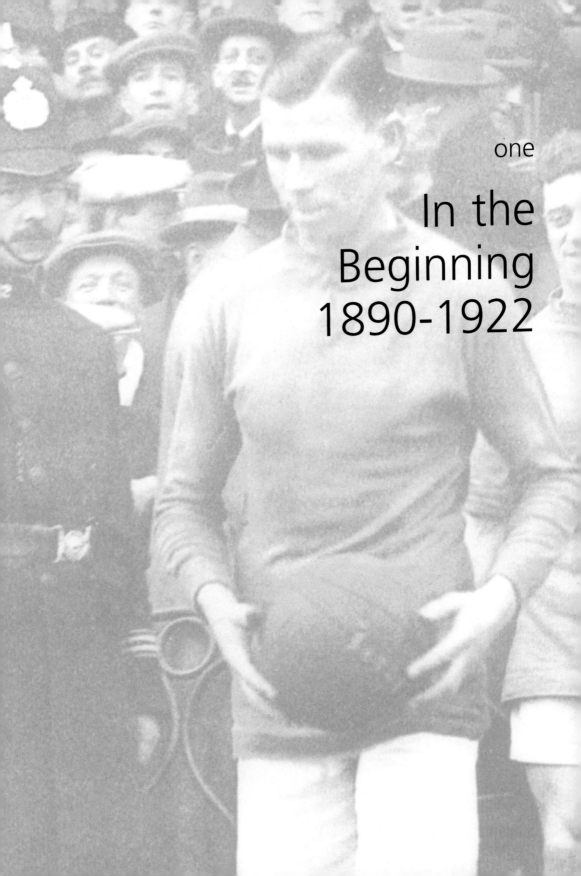

one

In the Beginning 1890-1922

Northfleet Invita, as they were originally known, played their first game on the Wombwell Hall estate on a site close to the Six Bells (pictured) in Old Perry Street on 8 November 1890. The side had began earlier in the year as a cricket team and turned its attention to football as autumn began. Nearly all teenagers, they played friendly matches – although the term was only a loose description as the games were described as crude affairs allowing hacking, scrimmaging, barging and occasionally punching. With no referees at any matches other than the top ones, the teams had to adjudicate all the decisions between themselves – which of course led to further arguments.

Gravesend United were formed in 1893 by a merger between Gravesend Ormonde who played at the Bat and Ball ground and Gravesend who played at Fairfields on the Overcliffe on a site behind what is now the Overcliffe Hotel (pictured) and bordered by St James Avenue and Lennox Avenue. The Shrimpers then became founder members of the Kent League in 1893/94 and moved on to their next ground in Pelham Road, now occupied by Gravesend Grammar School for Girls, a site the club lost in 1914 when it was requisitioned by the War Office before going to Kent CC. Although they were offered a ground share with Northfleet United they declined and did not play another game until 1932 – eighteen years after their previous match!

With football gradually becoming more organised Northfleet entered the Kent League for the first time in 1895/96 and won the championship at the first time of asking. Here, the team pose in traditional Victorian style with the trophy. The fourteen-man squad comprised Bundock (captain), Walker, King, Auld, Wright, Cullen, Ware, Grieves, Russell, Ferguson, Moody, McGregor, Hills and Cottam. Following this success it was time to move on, to Portland Meadows (now the huge Northfleet Cement Works) and then Huntley Meadows (now Huntley Avenue) where the ground ran parallel with the main railway line to London.

1897-98

First Division

	P	W	D	L	F	A	Pts
Southampton	22	18	1	3	53	18	37
Bristol City	22	13	7	2	67	33	33
Tottenham Hotspur	22	12	4	6	52	31	28
Chatham	22	12	4	6	50	34	28
Reading	22	8	7	7	39	31	23
New Brompton	22	9	4	9	37	37	22
Sheppey United	22	10	1	11	40	49	21
Gravesend United	22	7	6	9	28	39	20
Millwall Athletic	22	8	2	12	48	45	18
Swindon Town	22	7	2	13	36	48	16
Northfleet	22	4	3	15	29	60	11
Wolverton L & NW Railway	22	3	1	18	28	82	7

1900-01

First Division

	P	W	D	L	F	A	Pts
Southampton	28	18	5	5	58	26	41
Bristol City	28	17	5	6	54	27	39
Portsmouth	28	17	4	7	56	32	38
Millwall Athletic	28	17	2	9	55	32	36
Tottenham Hotspur	28	16	4	8	55	33	36
West Ham United	28	14	5	9	40	28	33
Bristol Rovers	28	14	4	10	46	35	32
Queens Park Rangers	28	11	4	13	43	48	26
Reading	28	8	8	12	24	25	24
Luton Town	28	11	2	15	43	49	24
Kettering	28	7	9	12	33	46	23
New Brompton	28	7	5	16	34	51	19
Gravesend United	28	6	7	15	32	85	19
Watford	28	6	4	18	24	52	16
Swindon Town	28	3	8	17	19	47	14

These two tables from the Southern League show how, at the dawn of the twentieth century, the local clubs were mixing with the elite of southern England. This was the time when a combined team would have been strong enough to challenge the best and would probably have been strong enough for a Football League place. It is worth noting that in 1900/01, when Tottenham famously became the first and last non-League team to win the FA Cup, Gravesend beat them 2-1 at Pelham Road in the league, although they suffered a 5-1 defeat at White Hart Lane.

An 1890 view of Stonebridge Road with the Plough public house and behind it the grand-looking Huggens College – a home for old folk demolished in the late 1960s and replaced by flats. In the foreground is Plough pond. If the camera had panned 90 degrees to the left where the ground now stands, water meadows would be seen all the way down to the river Thames 600 yards away. The cement company APCM (later Blue Circle) owned huge tracts of land and would provide the ground for the football club at a peppercorn rent fifteen years later because so many local people worked for them; it helped to develop good relations with the people. It was Northfleet's fourth and final ground and the first game was played on 2 September 1905 against East Ham in a friendly which Northfleet won 1-0. It would become one of the best and largest grounds in non-League football before its sad decline in the late twentieth century.

Gravesend United line up at their Pelham Road ground before taking on arch local rivals Northfleet United. The date is 18 March 1905 and the Shrimpers beat the Fleet (or Cementers, as they were also often called) 2-0 in a West Kent League game in front of a crowd of 3,000. From left to right, back row: H. Porter, C. Stapley, S. Parkinson, F. Obee, T. Penney, referee, R. Colquhoun. Front row: J. Seppitt, H. Mann, E. Parkinson, Sir Gilbert Parker MP, E. Mann, L. Stott, T. Smith.

GRAVESEND UNITED FOOTBALL CLUB.

GROUND:
Sports Ground, Pelham Road.

HEADQUARTERS:
15 Milton Road, Gravesend.

Dear Sir,

You are selected to play for the above Club on *Saturday*

next, the *23rd* day of *September* 190*5*, against

Maidstone United at *Maidstone* Kick-off *3.30* sharp.
Thames & Medway Combination

Yours truly,

J D Seppit

The Train leaves *Gravesend Central* Station at *2.18* sharp.

A postcard for Gravesend forward Len Stott informing him of his selection for the match at Maidstone on 23 September 1905. Len lived in Toronto Road, Tilbury, so would have caught the Tilbury–Gravesend ferry (then a very frequent service and the only means of getting from Essex to Kent without going via London) and after disembarking would have presumably strolled up Gravesend High Street and Windmill Street and met his teammates at what was then Gravesend Central Station.

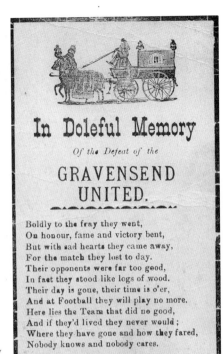

In Doleful Memory

Of the Defeat of the

GRAVENSEND
UNITED.

Boldly to the fray they went,
On honour, fame and victory bent,
But with sad hearts they came away,
For the match they lost to day.
Their opponents were far too good,
In fact they stood like logs of wood.
Their day is gone, their time is o'er,
And at Football they will play no more.
Here lies the Team that did no good,
And if they'd lived they never would ;
Where they have gone and how they fared,
Nobody knows and nobody cares.

This postcard was issued following another defeat for the Shrimpers. Although the date is unknown it was probably issued in the early years of the twentieth century.

Bill Jacques (1888-1925). Northfleet born Bill was the first outstanding player produced by Northfleet United. A fine goalkeeper, he moved to Coventry City in 1911 after helping the Fleet win both the Kent League and Kent Senior Cup. He then moved onto Tottenham where he was ever-present in the side that won the Second Division Championship in 1919/20 but missed out on their 1921 FA Cup triumph through injury. His poor health forced his retirement in 1923 after amassing 238 appearances for Spurs and he sadly died at Dartford in 1925 aged only thirty-six.

Charles Buchan (1891-1960), one of the legends of the first half of the twentieth century. Born in Plumstead, his career appeared to be going nowhere at Woolwich Arsenal and he signed for Northfleet in 1909 where he made an immediate impact, helping Northfleet to a hat-trick of trophies in his only season. Charles moved to Leyton and then on to Sunderland where he played from 1910 to 1924, making 380 appearances and scoring 209 goals. He won a League title and an FA Cup runners-up medal there and is still revered in the area as one of their all-time greats. He moved back down south to play for Arsenal between 1924 and 1927 and although by now a veteran he still scored 49 goals in 102 games, gaining a second FA Cup runners-up medal The England international retired after this to enjoy a second successful career as a sports journalist, first with the *News Chronicle* and then founding his own football magazine in 1951, the *Charles Buchan Football Monthly*. He died in the South of France in 1961.

Northfleet United produced their greatest team yet in 1909/10, completing a hat-trick of Kent League titles and a treble for the season by adding the Kent Senior Cup and the Thames and Medway Combination. Unfortunately, by the time this celebration photo was taken two key players – inside forward Charles Buchan and goalkeeper Bill Jacques – had moved on. Players only, from left to right, back row: Rogers, Fox, Quail. Middle row: Crowhurst, Williams, Kennedy, Jeacock, Hams. Front row: Nash, Myers, Sharpe. Sadly, both Kennedy and Myers were killed during the First World War.

Northfleet United recorded a fifth Kent League title in 1919/20. Players only, from left to right, back row: Evans, Seccombe, Good, Green, Gegus, Lawrence, Makepiece, Harbor. Front row: Daisley, Jewhurst, Tyler (captain).

Kent Senior Cup.

SPLENDID GAME AND RECORD GATE AT MAIDSTONE.

WILD ENTHUSIASM AT NORTHFLEET.

With the added "charm of the cup," imparted to the keen local rivalry that exists between Northfleet and Gravesend, it was small wonder, that, in spite of the dull threatening weather, huge crowds from both towns proceeded to Maidstone, there to see the final fight for possession of the trophy take place. The great majority made the journey by rail and the gate which amounted to £215, is a record for the cup ties at the Maidstone ground.

Bells and other musical instruments galore were on evidence everywhere while other paraphernalia in the form of coloured hats, umbrellas, favours, etc., were freely besprinkled amongst the huge crowd. All points of vantage were made use of and some excitement was caused when a branch of a tree broke and precipitated the occupant on top of one of the stands, fortunately for him, without injury.

Among the interested spectators were Mr. J. McKenna, vice-president of the Football Association, and Mr. Tom Watson, of Sunderland fame, and their opinion of the game: "Bright, crisp, healthy football" was an apt summary of the match.

The past performances of the teams, both in the Kent League and in their progress through the cup competition show the Cementers as the better team (these were published in last week's issue), but the Shrimper's mainly through the untiring zeal of the club's officials in finding new talent have greatly improved of late, and with a defence probably second to none in the Kent League had reasonable hopes of securing the victory. On the other hand, the Cementers were confident of victory, but as the very uncertainty of football is perhaps its greatest charm, the supporters of both clubs accompanied the teams and witnessed an attractive game, victory just going to the better side, and the score 2—1 just about representing the superiority. This was the first occasion on which the teams have met in the final. Northfleet may well be proud of their brilliant achievements in the football world, for with a scattered population of about 4,000 to draw from for support, the continued success that marks their efforts must surely be phenomenal for so small a town and speaks volumes for the businesslike way in which the work of the club is conducted by Councillor J. B. Lingham, vice-chairman K.C.F.A., and Chairman of the Club, whose name is almost synonymous with football and whose devoted labour and interest in the popular pastime has had no small part in the club's many successes. Mr. G. Blight, hon. treasurer, and Mr. F. Reynolds, the indefatigable secretary, who are loyally supported by a small, hard-working committee. Mr. T. Church, C.C., as president, takes a deep interest in the welfare of the club, while the social side of the game is greatly helped by a Ladies' Committee.

The train with the conquerors in streamed into the Northfleet station soon after 9 p.m. and here crowds had assembled to welcome them back, while the Northfleet Fire Brigade and engine were also waiting. Mounting the engine along with the team, the chairman held the cup aloft and then began a triumphal procession, headed by the Northfleet Silver Band playing suitable airs, through the main streets to the Hill returning to the Factory Club (headquarters), where the cup was filled and passed merrily round.

The populace gave vent to their great joy in many ways, which baffle description in fact, for the time being, Northfleet went mad.

After the match, Mr. H. A. Porter (Chairman K.C.F.A.) of Gravesend, who donned the losers' colours congratulated the teams on their play and the winners on their victory, although he said that, being a Gravesend man, he would have liked to have seen Gravesend win. Referring to the continued ill health of the president, Col. Griffiths for whom he was deputising, that afternoon, he wished him a speedy recovery to health, and presenting the cup to the Northfleet captain (J. Mason) asked him to call three cheers for the losers. Mrs. Porter then gracefully presented the medals to both teams. Mr. T. Church (president Northfleet Club) proposed a hearty vote of thanks to Mr. and Mrs. Porter, and Mr. Chalk (Gravesend) in seconding remarked that Mr. Porter was secretary of the Gravesend Club when they won the cup before. Three hearty cheers were then given. After these proceedings Mr. and Mrs. Porter were presented with a gold medal and brooch, respectively by Mr. J. B. Lingham on behalf of the members of the K.C.F.A.

The game opened at a fast pace and almost without interruption this state of affairs continued to the end, a fact that says much for the excellent condition of the players. It was a thrilling game to watch and Geggus, the Shrimpers' goalkeeper, gave a superb display, making glorious saves from Lawrence repeatedly. The "hero" of the match was Seccombe or as he is popularly known "little Sec," who was unquestionably one of the outstanding players of an excellent game. His sprightliness and dribbling throughout were absolutely great while he disconcerted the defence repeatedly. The play that lead to his goal was exceptionally brilliant and well merited the prolonged applause that greeted the materialising of his great effort. From thence onward "Seccombe's goal" was the theme of conversation. Receiving the ball towards the left of the field he worried his way by five opponents as one inspired, and with only Geggus to beat, in itself no mean performance, guided the ball into the net twenty-seven minutes from the start and gave his side the lead. It was brief, but characteristic of the player and undoubtedly one of the finest goals scored—a great goal worthy of a great occasion. By this goal Northfleet led at the interval. Eleven minutes from the restart Sharp beautifully placed the ball at the feet of Lawrence who cleverly dribbled through the defence and with a hard drive sent the ball to the left of the net well out of the reach of Geggus. With nineteen minutes to go Armitage taking the ball on the run sent in a tremendous shot from fairly long distance, but although Henry partly gathered it the "screw" on it caused it to spin over his arm into the net and Armitage had the honour of scoring the first goal against the Fleets in the competition. The effect of this goal was to cause both teams to redouble their efforts and the game went on at a rare pace and the Shrimpers were urged on to get the equaliser but over anxiety prevented them utilising an excellent chance and no more scoring took place.

In the early stages of the game Gravesend had the better of the midfield play but their forwards were weak compared with the other part of the team. Thorndyke easily tested Henry with some long grounders, while several shots went wide of the mark. Waggott was prominent on several occasions but failed to dash through, while Armitage always ready to dash through, proved a thorn in the opponents' defence. Thorndike, in the first few minutes was responsible for some clever work once putting Williams in a grand position and himself just missing the net by inches.

The Fleets' forwards were more dangerous than Gravesend's, although they found Dodd a rare stumbling block in attempting to penetrate an almost impassable barrier. But Blackburn who was suffering from an injury and was reluctant to play, missed two fine chances of scoring from some of Myers magnificent centres, and this made him slower than usual and neutralised to some extent the efficiency of the line. Lawrence played in brilliant style, in keeping his wings up, and in testing Geggus with a large number of excellent shots, which the custodian dealt with in masterly style. His most praiseworthy effort being when he brought down a dangerous shot from just under the crossbar, while another equally praiseworthy save was from a dangerous centre by Myers. The latter player gave a fine exposition on the wing, and he and Seccombe combining splendidly, while Seager plied his centre with excellent passes. The half-backs on each side were in fine fettle and kept their forwards going from end to end which was the cause of much exciting play. Tyler, perhaps, was the best of six clever players, being the more polished in his methods, but Jarvis ran him very closely. The backs formed a sturdy defence, with Dodd playing the better game for at times he was hard pressed and came out with flying colours. A curious incident in the first half occurred. Mason apparently handled the ball and Dodd near the halfway line caught the ball evidently thinking he was going to have a free kick, but the whistle had not gone. When it did, however, to Dodd's chagrin, it was against him.

Henry with the one exception shaped splendidly, at times throwing himself full length in protecting his charge, and with experience should make a good goalkeeper.

A great feature of the game was the sporting spirit in which the players engaged in a stern battle, while throughout the game very few free kicks were taken, and these were generally for a technical offence only. The effect of this was to provide pleasure for the spectators while the earnestness of the players and the high standard of play attained at times marks this final as one of the best contests in the history of the cup.

This makes the third time that Northfleet have held the cup, the previous times being: 1895-6, 1909-10, while Gravesend were the proud holders in 1897-8 and 1899-1900.

The teams were:—

Northfleet: Henry; Mason, Goodhind; Nash, Sharp, Tyler; Blackburn, Seager, Lawrence, Seccombe, Myers.

Gravesend: Geggus; Wood, Dodd; Massey, Jarvis, Childs; Williams, Armitage, Thorndike, Waggott, Walters.

Referee: Mr. P. C. Black. Linesmen: Messrs. E. H. Warts and J. C. Hubble.

KENT LEAGUE TABLE.

	P.	W.	D.	L.	F.	A.	P.
Millwall R.	23	16	4	3	59	16	36
Crystal Palace R.	20	15	3	4	74	27	33
Northfleet	21	12	5	4	47	30	27
Dartford	21	11	3	7	47	41	25
Royal Naval Depot	21	9	5	7	53	27	23
Gillingham R.	20	9	5	10	36	55	23
Sittingbourne	20	8	6	8	43	11	22
Maidstone	21	7	7	7	39	34	21
Chatham	20	7	5	8	46	42	20
Gravesend	21	7	5	9	39	41	19
Margate	18	7	5	8	28	28	18
Sheppey	20	5	4	10	26	33	16
Bromley	20	4	6	12	32	47	14
Cray Wanderers	20	5	2	16	30	54	12
Rochester	21	3	1	15	27	69	11

The 1912/13 Kent Senior Cup final provided the only occasion when the two local rivals met in a major final. An estimated 10,000 watched the final at Maidstone, which saw Northfleet win a hard-fought tussle by two goals to one against a gallant Gravesend side.

PRICE TWOPENCE.

Official Programme.

Kent County Football Association.

SENIOR CUP.—FINAL TIE.

Easter Monday, March 28th, 1921,
Kick off 3.30.

NORTHFLEET.

R.   Goal.   L.
JOYCE.
1.
Backs.
BARNFATHER.   O'CONOR.
2   3
Half-Backs.
DAISLEY.   SWAYNE   ING.
4   5   6
Forwards.
BARNETT   SECCOMBE.   LAYTON.   DAY.   HARBER.
7   8   9   10   11

COPESTAKE   HUMPHREY, D.   EACOCK.   LAURENCE.   WILLIAMSON.
12   13   14   15   16
Forwards.
WELLS.   PAGE.   HALL.
17   18   19
Half-Backs.
CHALKLEY.   COLLYER.
20   21
Backs.
PLEASANTS.
22
Goal.
L.   R.

(left margin, vertical:) Linesman.—Serg. Maj. FORD, R.M.L.I.

(right margin, vertical:) Linesman—J. C. HUBBLE.

RAMSGATE.
Referee—A. J. RULE.

The Cup and Medals will be presented by Mrs. FEHR, wife of the President K.C.F.A.

Dickinson, Printer, High Street, Maidstone.

Above left: A large crowd, estimated at more than 10,000, packed into Maidstone to see Northfleet overcome Ramsgate 1-0, a seventieth-minute Arthur Seccombe goal deciding the issue and giving the Fleet a fourth Kent Senior Cup triumph.

Above right: Arthur Seccombe, a real Fleet legend. From the time he joined the club from local football as an eighteen-year-old in 1911 until his retirement in 1926 as a thirty-three-year-old he played more games (450) and scored more goals (250) than any other player. His medal collection, comprising a record six Kent Senior Cups, two Kent League Championships and one Kent League Cup, highlighted a brillant career.

The Northfleet end of Stonebridge Road is packed to see the home side beat Sheppey United 4-1 in the first qualifying round of the FA Cup on 9 October 1920. Fleet went on to beat Worthing 5-0 in the next round before exiting at Maidstone by the same scoreline. Apart from minor improvements, the Northfleet end would remain the same until the early 1950s when a large covered terrace was built – one of the largest stands in non-League football. Sadly, the years took their toll, culminating in the stand's closure by the safety authorities in 2005. It was allowed to be reopened with a considerably reduced capacity and at the time of writing the possibility of installing several hundred seats in the front rows was being investigated.

two

The Tottenham Connection 1923-1945

Billy Lane

Bill Lane (1904–1985). In 1923 an historic agreement was made between Northfleet and Tottenham Hotspur, providing the Fleet with a batch of promising Spurs youngsters each season to help knock the rough edges off the youngsters and give them vital experience in the rough, tough world of non-League football. Bill Lane was in the first intake of 1923/24 and had a memorable single season; although only fourth place was attained in the league the club swept to victory in the Kent Senior Cup and Kent League Cup, while a draw with Gillingham earned them a half share in the Kent Senior Shield. The centre forward was never able to pin down a regular place in the Spurs side and went on to have successful spells at Watford, Brentford and Bristol City. After the Second World War he moved into management with good results at both Guildford and Brighton. In 1961 he came full circle and ended up back where it had all started for him at Stonebridge Road. He was in charge during the legendary FA Cup run of 1962/63 but the club's league form was desperately disappointing, ending in relegation, and Bill resigned at the end of that season.

Bill Edrich

Bill Whatley

Vic Buckingham

Above left: Vic Buckingham (1915-1995). Greenwich-born Buckingham signed for Northfleet in 1934, playing at both left-back and left half in his single season which saw him play a solid role in achieving a Kent League and Cup double. He went on to play 204 games for Spurs before moving abroad to coach, later returning to manage West Bromwich Albion and Fulham.

Above right: Arthur Rowe (1906-1993). The Tottenham-born centre half played four seasons for Northfleet between 1925 and 1929 in one of the Fleet's most successful spells. He went on to play 182 times for Spurs before becoming player-manager at Chelmsford where he had outstanding success, taking them to a Southern League and Cup double in 1945/46. Moving back to Spurs, he had even greater success with his legendary 'push and run' side winning the Second and First Divisions of the Football League in successive seasons. He is pictured in his Spurs managerial days.

Opposite below, left: Bill Edrich (1916-1986). Better known as a brilliant cricketer, playing 39 Test matches for England, Bill played on the left wing for Northfleet in 1934/35, helping them to the Kent League and Cup double. He moved on to Spurs but managed only 20 appearances and concentrated more and more on his cricket with Middlesex and England.

Opposite below, right: Bill Whatley (1912-1974). The Ebbw Vale born full-back played at Northfleet in 1931/32 helping the club to a Kent League and Cup double. He went on to play more than 200 games for Spurs and was capped for Wales. He returned to Stonebridge Road in 1954 as manager but sadly his youth policy proved disastrous as his string of youngsters proved ill-equipped for the Southern League and he was sacked before the year was out.

George Ludford (1915-2001). The free scoring Barnet-born centre forward became a goalscoring legend in his three years at Stonebridge Road (1933-1936). Only 10st in weight and 5ft 6in tall, he needed to be fleet of foot against the bruising Kent League defenders he came up against and the fact he blitzed an amazing 104 league and cup goals in 1935/36 showed just how effective he was. He won two Kent League titles and a Kent League Cup winners' medal before returning to Spurs, where he was never able to really nail down a regular place, making 75 appearances in a long spell at White Hart Lane that spanned the Second World War. He later managed and became a director at Enfield.

Albert Ringrose

Bert Ringrose (1916-1968). Edmonton-born Bert achieved a unique record by being the only player to perform for Northfleet United (1934-1936), Tottenham Hotspur (1937-1939) and Gravesend & Northfleet (1946-1947). An accomplished full-back, he played in the very first game for the newly formed Gravesend & Northfleet in 1946.

Above left: Ron Burgess (1917-2005). The Welsh-born future captain of Spurs and Wales destined to lead the 'push and run' team to successive Second and First Division League titles in 1949/50 and 1950/51 quickly established himself at Northfleet during his two-year spell (1936-38). Playing at wing half, he collected Kent League, Kent League Cup and Kent Senior Cup honours before making the first of 297 appearances for Spurs in February 1939.

Above right: Freddie Cox (1920-1973). Reading-born Freddie played on the right wing for Northfleet between 1936 and 1938 at a time when many promising future Spurs stars were making their way at Stonebridge Road. He collected winners' medals in the Kent League, two Kent League Cups and the Kent Senior Cup. He managed 99 games for Tottenham before becoming one of the rare Spurs players to move over to Arsenal, later moving on to West Bromwich Albion. He went on to manage Bournemouth and Gillingham.

Right: Bill Nicholson (1919-2004). Scarborough-born Bill was the most famous player to don the red shirt of Northfleet and his spell between 1936 and 1938 provided him with his first taste of success, winning the Kent League and Kent Senior Cup before starting on a long 314-appearance Spurs career that was topped by his legendary spell as manager from 1958 to 1974.

BILL NICHOLSON

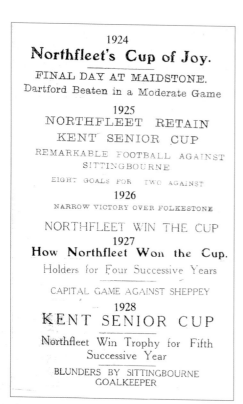

Above left: Between 1924 and 1928, Northfleet United won the Kent Senior Cup a record five times in succession, a record that still stands today. These were the days of 10,000-strong crowds for the final, when all Kent stopped and the winning side were given civic receptions by the grateful home borough. The victories were achieved against Dartford 1-0, Sittingbourne 8-2, Folkstone 1-0, Sheppey 1-0 and Sittingbourne 3-1. Two players, forwards Bell and Pilcher, played in all five finals.

Above right: A record fifth successive Kent Senior Cup victory was recorded on Easter Monday 1928 with a 3-1 victory over Sittingbourne.

Opposite: Stonebridge Road in 1932, when the main stand was still in its full glory. On the Stonebridge Road side of the ground is the small stand rescued from the ailing Rosherville Gardens, complete with ornate pillaring, which stood on the ground from 1909 until it was dismantled in 1953. Both goal sides look pretty basic, although there was some terracing. But one thing never changes, as the groundsman can be seen on the pitch, grafting away.

Northfleet United line-up in 1936/37, the season they were destined to take the Kent League title for the tenth time overall and the third in a row. From left to right, back row: S. Levett (hon. secretary), W.J. Treadwell (vice-chairman), A. Smith, L. Hiscoke, H. Leonard, G. Barron, R. Burgess, J. Roberts, C. Revell, J. Lingham (president), W.H. Hardy (chairman). Front row: J. Anderson (trainer), F. Cox, G. Skinner, J. Coxford, C. Trailor, D. Coulston, A. Day.

A first taste of success for future stars Bill Nicholson and Ron Burgess as they celebrate a hard-fought 1938 Kent Senior Cup final victory, 2-1 against Dover. Sadly it was to be the tenth and last time the club won the competition. Players only, from left to right, back row: Nicholson, Revell, Barron, Coxford (with cup), Skinner, Trailor, Burgess, Evans. Front row: Coulston, Day, Roberts.

TOTTENHAM HOTSPUR PLAYERS WHO MADE FOOTBALL LEAGUE APPEARANCES(IN BRACKETS) AND THEIR NORTHFLEET UNITED CAREER SPANS.

Joe Allen (1)   1932-34
Wally Alsford (81) 1929-30
Les Bennett (272) 1938-39
Vic Buckingham (204) 1934-35
Ron Burgess (297) 1936-38
Fred Channell (95) 1932-33
Freddie Cox (99) 1936-38
Alf Day (13)   1928-31
Ted Ditchburn (418) 1938-39
Bill Edrich (20)   1934-35
Albert Evans (5) 1926-27
Arthur Hitchins (35) 1934-36
Percy Hooper (97) 1933-35
Les Howe (165)   1928-32
Doug Hunt (17)   1932-34
Jack Illingworth (10)   1927-29
Charles Jones (18)   1932-34
Eddie King (1)   1933-34
Billy Lane (26)   1923-24

David Levane (8)   1931-32
George Ludford (75)   1933-36
Les Medley (150)   1937-39
Johny Morrison (133)   1931-32
Bill Nicholson (314)   1936-38
Taffy O'Callaghan (252) 1925-27
Ernie Phypers (30)   1933-34
Jack Richardson (38)   1924-25
Bert Ringrose (10)   1934-36
Tommy Roe (7)   1924-25
Arthur Rowe (182)   1925-29
Arthur Sanders (13)   1923-30
Fred Sargent (93)   1934-35
George Skinner (1)   1937-39
Harry Skit (212)   1923-24
Sid Tickridge (95)   1939-40
Cyril Trailor (11)   1936-39
Bill Whatley (226)   1931-32

Above: A list of the thirty-seven players who played for Northfleet United and then moved on to play in the Football League for Tottenham Hotspur.

Right: Les Bennett (1918–1999). Born at Wood Green, this clever inside forward completed only one full season at Northfleet, 1938/39. Les was a member of the team that played Northfleet's very last match before war broke out in September 1939. After the war he became an important member of the Spurs side that won Second and First Division titles in successive seasons, scoring 104 goals in 272 games before enjoying a brief spell at West Ham United prior to retirement.

Les Bennett

Ted Ditchburn

Ted Ditchburn (1921-2005). Gillingham-born Ted moved to the Northfleet area while still a schoolboy and, after quickly giving up the idea of following his father into the boxing ring, became a brilliant goalkeeper, moving on to Spurs after a highly impressive 1938/39 season at Northfleet. He made 418 appearances for Tottenham and played for England. He was the last playing link between Northfleet and Tottenham, making his last appearance for Spurs in 1958.

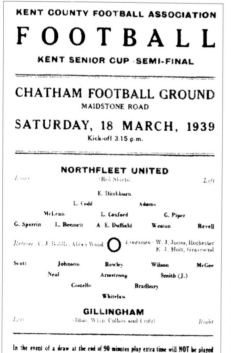

KENT COUNTY FOOTBALL ASSOCIATION

FOOTBALL

KENT SENIOR CUP SEMI-FINAL

CHATHAM FOOTBALL GROUND
MAIDSTONE ROAD

SATURDAY, 18 MARCH, 1939
Kick-off 3.15 p.m.

NORTHFLEET UNITED

(Red Shirts)

E. Ditchburn

L. Codd   Adams

McLean   L. Coxford   C. Piper

G. Sperrin   L. Bennett   A. E. Duffield   Weston   Revell

Referee: C.J. Babb, Abbey Wood   Linesmen: W. J. Jones, Rochester
F. J. Holt, Gravesend

Scott   Johnson   Bewley   Wilson   McGee

Neal   Armstrong   Smith (J.)

Costello   Bradbury

Whitelaw

GILLINGHAM

(Blue, White Collars and Cuffs)

In the event of a draw at the end of 90 minutes play extra time will NOT be played

H. S. Godfrey, Printer, High Street, Rainham, Kent

Northfleet *v.* Gillingham in the Kent Senior Cup semi-final of 1938/39 was the Fleet's last ever game in the competition as the Gills won 2-0 and even the highly promising Ted Ditchburn in goal could do nothing about it. Les Bennett, like Ditchburn destined to win a Football League Championship medal a decade later, and future Charlton star Charlie Revill also played for Fleet.

Sid Tickridge

Above left: Sid Tickridge (1923-). Stepney-born Sid came to Stonebridge Road as a sixteen-year-old in 1939 and played at full-back in the club's last ever match before war was declared. He was the final Spurs player to come off the Northfleet conveyer belt. After the war he played nearly 100 times for Spurs before moving on to Chelsea and later Brentford.

Above right: Joe Lingham (1870-1943). Very much Mr Northfleet United, Joe was a founder member of the club as a twenty-year-old player. His building company at 1 The Hill, Northfleet made him a rich man and also benefited the club as it was they who erected the main stand, opened in 1920. Joe became chairman of the club in 1906, a role he kept for most of his life before becoming president. He was also a prominent member of the Kent County Football Association and Northfleet – and football – lost a true friend on his death in December 1943.

'FLEET'S VICTORY AT DARTFORD

Second Half Superiority.

BENNETT THE STAR.

After being a goal behind for half-an-hour, Northfleet United defeated Dartford by 4—3 in a Kent League fixture at Watling-street on Saturday.

Dartford deservedly took the lead in the 18th minute, and then the 'Fleet's faithful followers had to wait until early in the second half before they could cheer the equaliser.

It was a commentary on the close and often very keen struggle that both these goals came after free-kicks for fouls.

Twenty-one minutes after the interval Northfleet were leading by 3—1. Sitting pretty, their supporters thought!

But no, for Dartford kept the game alive by narrowing the margin eighteen minutes from the finish.

EXCITING EXCHANGES

Northfleet met this challenge with a fourth goal (nine minutes to go). Then their defence blundered once more and the dashing "Darts" again restricted the Cementers' advantage. It was all most exciting.

In fact the game will remain in the memory of all who saw it because of its fluctuating phases—but chiefly, of course, because it was what it was—the last Dartford — Northfleet match before war was declared.

One wonders how long will elapse before these near neighbours and old rivals meet again?

It was significant that five of the seven goals were scored down the slope towards the London-road end of the ground.

Northfleet fielded the team that thrashed Lloyd's a week earlier.

TWO FACTORS.

But two factors prevented the Reds repeating that very good display—and these were the far stronger opposition and the rough state of the pitch. This was a real handicap.

The teams were as follows:—

Dartford: W. Pearson; A. Golding, R. Jury; C Wilson, S. Randle, F. Couchman; G Gray, R. Stanton, F. Dunham, R. Collins, D. Dowsett.

Northfleet United: S. Raven; S. Tickridge, H. Rayment; Hiscoke, A. Holmes, Piper; J. Dowers, Bennett, J. Browne, Roberts, W. Simpson.

Referee: Mr. J. Weller.

Roberts beat Randle for choice of ends and set Dartford to defend the Watling-street goal.

The first shot came from Roberts but Pearson got the ball away and Dartford at once replied. Stanton shooting wide.

Both sides missed good-looking chances

in the following minutes. Couchman missed in his stride and both Simpson and Browne failed at the other end.

Just later Browne, supplied with a perfect pass by Bennett, should have given Northfleet the lead. Instead he ballooned the ball "miles" over the bar and a fresh ball had to be brought into use.

It was soon after this that Dartford went ahead. Dowsett was fouled by Hiscoke, and Jury hit the crossbar with the free-kick. Collins secured the rebound and scored. Eighteen minutes had gone.

In the end-to-end play which followed for the rest of the first half several chances were allowed to drift. In a spirited attack Browne again shot too high and Bennett went very near with a header from Simpson's well-placed flag-kick.

PIPER PROMINENT.

Randle and Browne had many a tussle and each was penalised in turn. The long-striding Piper was often prominent.

As the interval approached Northfleet intensified their efforts to equalise and the home custodian did well to save from Dowers and clear a corner from Simpson. A shot from Bennett was blocked, rather luckily, at the cost of another corner.

A brilliant free-kick by Roberts gave Northfleet the leveller three minutes after the resumption. Randle held off the eager young Browne and this was the result. The way Roberts "hit" that free-kick was reminiscent of Jack Cosford at his best.

CLEVER SOLO EFFORT.

Seven minutes later Bennett brought the house down with a really very clever solo effort. He beat three opponents before shooting past the goalkeeper. This was Leslie Bennett at his brilliant best.

Foolish "hands" irritated the already overwrought spectators before Browne, after a Piper-Bennett movement, again placed the ball far too high.

Northfleet were well on top now, and the home goal had several escapes before Simpson scored No. 3 after the goalie had pushed out a shot from Browne.

After this a Collin's header went near, and in the 27th minute the same player registered Dartford's second success just when a goal was required to keep the game alive.

And very much alive it remained till the end.

Browne obtained the 'Fleet's fourth goal when only nine minutes remained.

Dartford's third was a gift for Dowsett —after Holmes had foolishly passed back to Raven.

After the match the Northfleet President (Mr. J. B. Lingham, J.P.), accompanied by other officials of the Club, went to the dressing room to say au-revoir to Jimmy Anderson and the players and to wish them good luck during the War.

Left: Northfleet played their last ever game on 2 September 1939, just a day before war was declared, and it was fitting that the opposition for the Kent League game was the old enemy Dartford. The Fleet won 4-3 to make it three wins out of three for the season – sadly, that was to be it. Gravesend United survived seven years longer and added a third Kent Senior Cup to their honours list in a severely truncated 1944 competition. They played their last game at Ramsgate in April 1946, losing 2-0.

Below: Central Avenue was the fourth ground of Gravesend United following Fairfields, Pelham Road and, for a brief season-long stay following their re-formation in 1932, Milton Barracks. They moved into the Central Avenue ground in 1933 and remained there until their end in 1946. This photograph is taken from where one of the goals once stood, with the opposing goal now swallowed up by housing. The main stand stood on the left and remained there until the late 1970s while the ground was in use by Gravesend Rugby Club. The changing rooms were in the Central Hotel (now the Ascot Arms), out of view on the right.

Together
at Last
1946-1949

ANDREW N. WILSON
CHELSEA

Above: A new beginning as Gravesend & Northfleet line up before their very first match on 31 August 1946 for a Southern League match against the previous season's runners-up Hereford United. The Bulls were to be brushed aside by a 3-0 margin as the new era got off to an exciting start in front of a 6,000 crowd.

Left: Andy Wilson (1896-1973) was the club's first manager. Born in Newmains, Lanarkshire, he began as a centre forward with Cambuslang Rangers and the sheer weight of goals he scored quickly got him noticed and he moved south to Middlesbrough. His next move was even further south to Chelsea for a record £6,000 fee in 1923. He played 14 times for Scotland, scoring 17 goals – the best ratio of any Scottish player. He moved on to Walsall, where he later became manager. He made light of a serious injury to his arm sustained in the First World War, although the handicap gradually got worse and he was rarely seen without a protective glove. He later played bowls for his adopted country. After a relatively successful first season at Gravesend & Northfleet in 1946/47, disagreements with the board of directors began to emerge and he departed in the close season. His son Jim played for the Fleet during that first season before later moving to Watford.

Ken Horrigan (1919-1989). Gravesend-born Ken began his senior career at Carlisle before returning to Kent and taking over as captain for the 1947/48 season. He was a driving force for the club at right half, taking them to the finals of the Kent Senior Cup and Kent Senior Shield – sadly both were lost, to Gillingham and Margate respectively. After that single season, when he played 51 games and scored 3 goals, Ken moved into Kent League football with Ashford and Gillingham whilst continuing to live and work in Gravesend.

Clancy McDermott was a flame-haired Irishman who played in the club's first two seasons, amassing 80 appearances without scoring a goal from his left half position. He moved to Chelmsford City in 1948.

Sid Bidewell (1918-). Born in Wymondham, Sid played at left-back in Gravesend's very first match. He had begun his career with St Albans and moved on to play for Wealdstone and then Chelsea before the Second World War intervened. Sid played two seasons for the Fleet, amassing 83 appearances. He moved on to Chelmsford in 1948.

Gravesend & Northfleet cartoon, 1947/48.

Above left: Cyril Griggs, another local youngster who was Fleet's first regular goalkeeper, making a total of 81 appearances between 1946 and 1948.

Above right: Vic Hayes was a full-back who made 51 appearances in his two seasons before moving to Bedford. He later returned as coach in 1960/61 and stayed in the area afterwards.

Left: A tense 2-0 victory over Dartford set the scene for a memorable 1948/49 Kent Senior Cup final with Gillingham.

GILBERT ALDOUS, Northfleet born and former Bromley back, is well-liked captain of United.

Above: Gilbert Aldous receives the Kent Senior Cup from R.J. Rule, chairman of the KCFA, after Gravesend & Northfleet finally overcame Gillingham in a second replay. The fact that two of those games took place in the Gills' own Priestfield back yard made the achievement even more creditable. The incredible saga began with a 2-2 draw at Maidstone, watched by 8,250 people; because of demand the replay had to be switched to the largest Kent ground at Priestfield, which was justified by a record-breaking 16,733 crowd to watch a 1-1 draw. Then came the third game and the deadlock was broken in front of 12,633 as the Fleet won 2-0.

Left, above and below: Northfleet-born brothers Stan and Gilbert Aldous were vital cogs in the side that won the Fleet their first trophy: the 1948/49 Kent Senior Cup. Both started their senior careers at Bromley before switching to their home-town team in 1948. Stan played 111 times and scored 3 goals before moving to Leyton Orient where he had further success. He returned as manager (unpaid) in 1967 and played a couple of games as a player – the second oldest to play for Fleet. Gilbert played 76 times and also scored 3 times before suffering a serious injury on Boxing Day 1949 while playing Dartford. He was later given a benefit game and subsequently embarked upon a comeback with Kent League club Ramsgate.

STAN ALDOUS Leyton Orient

KENT SENIOR CUP FINAL—2nd REPLAY

Gravesend United's win after dour struggle

Holder's attack faltered on rugged defence

By "TOWNSMAN"

Gillingham, 0; Gravesend and Northfleet, 2.

TIP your hats to one of the strongest and most rugged defences in the Southern League.

It belongs to Gravesend and Northfleet United and, because of that, on Wednesday evening at Priestfield Stadium, they beat the homesters, Gillingham, to win the coveted Kent Senior Cup for the first time in their history.

Gillingham were the better footballing side, but their fast-moving attack got no change out of a defence that never let up and was rarely caught out of position.

It was a game of contrasting styles. Time and again the Gillingham attack, moving with precision and ably prompted by the halves, swept down on the Gravesend goal.

ROCK-LIKE DEFENCE

Each time they were driven back. The challengers' defence was rock steady and solid.

Many defences would have wilted under such combined pressure, but United's stood firm and such good cover did goalie Gould get that he was not often in trouble. Only one shot nearly beat him.

This was when Kingsnorth, in an effort to level the goal he had scored for Gravesend, let fly a beauty. Gould was pleased to push this one round. Cat-like in his movements, uncanny in anticipation, he made the rest look easy.

But Gravesend should have made the game safe in the first half.

After nine minutes a Baldwin-Wipfler move gave Hawkins a chance. His shot hit an upright with Burke beaten.

Later, Gravesend's leader cleverly drew the defence, beat Burke, but then fired over and wide of an open net!

Just before the break—no score—he "blinded" wide. This was real hard luck for a persevering leader.

GILLS BEAT THEMSELVES

At the interval betting was on Gillingham. They always looked better but never seemed able to get there. In short, they beat themselves.

They started off, however, as though they were going to cakewalk matters, but Williams, a shrewd leader who had too much to do, saw his header arrested by Gould's cross-bar. After that Aldous (S.) stuck to him closer than a long-lost brother.

Then, at the other end, Hawkins burst through and was allowed to proceed by the referee. He fired in a shot that entered the net via an upright, but the "goal" was disallowed.

After 55 minutes Gravesend went ahead. It was tragedy for Gillingham. Wipfler crossed a good pass to Wakeman, who had been having some stern duels with the ever-watchful Marks. This time the winger got the better of Marks and returned the ball to Wipfler. Firing into a crowd of players, he saw KINGSNORTH deflect the shot past Burke.

How strange it was that in all of the three games a player had scored against his own side! Gravesend, in the final and first replay, did it on each occasion.

Gillingham, in an effort to draw level, made forward switches, but still that rugged, dogged defence of United's came out on top.

Evergreen Wilson and young Briggs did all they knew. Former Spurs player, Williams, roamed and worked. All to no effect.

WAKEMAN HURT

Then, after Wakeman had been reduced to a hobbling passenger through a knee injury, came curtains for the holders.

Eight minutes to go, Deevey swung across a beautiful centre HAWKINS was waiting, and this time he made no mistake, rounding Kingsnorth and beating Burke from close range.

It was all over and Gravesend had won the Cup for the first time.

Let us then give them full marks. Although not as polished as Gillingham, they once again proved themselves a full 90-minute team.

Their defence was great, and in it, as the outstanding man, was centre-half Stan Aldous, with the rest very, very close on his heels.

Forward, Gravesend did not have the craft of Gillingham, but Wipfler was always a box of tricks. Hawkins should not be dismayed. He, like the rest, never gave up. In fact a fine all-round display and a worthy victory.

CUP PRESENTED

Cup and medals were presented by Alderman R. W. Rule, J.P., Chairman, K.C.F.A. Council.

Gravesend and Northfleet Utd.: Gould; Aldous (G.), Chambers; Busby, Aldous (S.), Dimmock; Wakeman, Deevey, Hawkins, Baldwin, Wipfler.

Gillingham: Burke; Dorling, Marks; Boswell, Kingsnorth, Piper; Warsap, Wilson, Williams, Carr; Briggs.

Above: The amazing three-match marathon that broke all records for the Kent Senior Cup final was finally decided in Fleet's favour on 31 August 1949. The need for a second replay meant that the game had to be carried into the 1949/50 season.

Above right: Roy Butler was the first Fleet player to score four goals in a game, achieving this in an 8-2 victory over Sittingbourne in the Kent Senior Shield. He had a fine goal ratio of 39 goals in 57 outings in his 1946-1948 Fleet career. He later played for Dartford, Tonbridge and Chelmsford and had a successful car sales business in Strood. Roy died in 2001.

Right: Wing half Ted Dimmock was one of the unsung heroes of the team that beat Gillingham to take the Kent Senior Cup in 1949. He made 79 appearances and scored 2 goals in his spell at the club between 1948 and 1951.

A 1949/50 drawing from the excellent but short-lived *Sporting Mirror*. One mystery: why the black and white outfit?

Gravesend Council held a reception at the town hall for the club after their Kent Senior Cup victory in 1949. Captain Gilbert Aldous stands proudly next to the mayor with other members of the team, club officials and the mayoress.

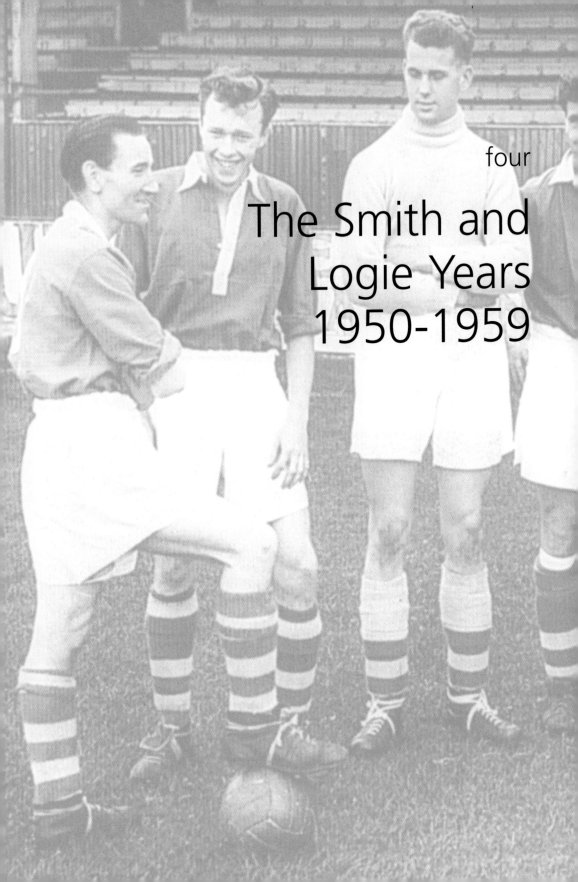

four

The Smith and Logie Years 1950-1959

New player-manager Cliff Edwards looks confident with his 1950/51 side but it was to be a disappointing campaign that saw the team finish eighteenth out of twenty-three sides in the Southern League. From left to right, back row: Ted Harston (trainer), Sam Chambers, Bert Hawkins, Jim Deevey, Tommy James, Percy Skinner, George Baldwin, Tom Peters, Cyril Gould. Front row: Les Gore, Tug Wilson, Cliff Edwards, Eddie Viles, George Fullbrook.

1953 Kent Senior Cup winning side
Back Row: Bill McEwan, Ted Harston (Trainer), Charlie Carroll, Jack Flockhart, Tom Baker,
Bill Longdon, Jim Peevey, Unkown, Fred Blowers, Harold Merrison (Director), John Rigg (Director),
Sam Chambers, Bert Hawkins.
Front Row: F. Stevens (Director), Ken Jones, Len Wakeman, Kevin Clarke,
Arthur Norris-Telling (Chairman), Gordon Loukes, Jack Winter, Arthur Rothwell (Driector)

Above and below: The 1952/53 team which won a second Kent Senior Cup with a 2-1 victory over local rivals Dartford, captured in both cartoon and photographic form.

Opposite left: Fred Blowers was a local goalkeeper who made 73 appearances in two spells with the club between 1952 and 1955. Fred later played more Southern League football for Dartford and Tonbridge.

Opposite right: Bert Hawkins (1923-1982). The Lambeth-born centre forward was the club's leading scorer for nearly fifty years and still holds the record of the most goals in a match – seven against Hastings in 1950. His 125 goals in 224 games came in two spells: 1947-1951, and then, after a relatively unsuccessful spell at Leyton Orient, 1952-1953.

DICK ROCHE.

Dick Roche became Fleet's surprise fourth manager in 1951. The forty-five-year-old schoolteacher was a surprise appointment, his main achievement being to produce a string of talented youngsters in youth football. He remained for a year before resigning.

Bill McEwan

Bill McEwan (1914-1991). Glasgow-born Bill was thirty-seven when he joined Fleet in 1951 but still had plenty of life in him, producing some fine displays in the outside right and centre forward positions. He played in the Kent Senior Cup victory over Dartford in 1953 and by the time he retired in 1954 he had played 108 games and scored 34 times.

KENT COUNTY
FOOTBALL ASSOCIATION

PRIESTFIELD STADIUM, PRIESTFIELD ROAD, GILLINGHAM

Easter Monday, 6th April 1953   Kick Off 3.15 p.m.

Official Programme

PRICE — — — TWOPENCE

Kent Senior Cup Final Tie

DARTFORD
v
GRAVESEND & NORTHFLEET

Senior Cup Comments

Traditionally Kent Football fought for the cup on each Easter, and though the complex character of the game in these advanced days has had the effect of leaving an over growing spate of important soccer events to be decided in the remaining weeks of the season, nothing quite attains to the status and prestige of the final tie of the County Senior Cup. To-day's encounter is the 59th in the history of the Competition, a long line of memorable contests unbroken except for the two World Wars, ranging from the comparatively modest finales of half a century ago on the old Mall ground at Faversham, through the 40 glorious years of achievement at Maidstone, and now on the third occasion of a new era on the stage of this Stadium at Priestfield Road, placed at the disposal of the County Association by the Directors of the Gillingham F.C.

This afternoon's battle is one between old contenders for the blue riband of senior football in Kent and both clubs have had a big part in adding lustre to their individual accomplishments and to the glory and distinction of the Competition itself. One may, I think, fairly regard the present Gravesend and Northfleet Club as the direct successors of the redoubtable Northfleet United of pre-war seasons. Official records credit them with 10 outright victories dating back to 1895-96 season. This is a record of triumph well ahead of any claimed by any other club in the County. But Dartford, too, have given the contest colour and distinction over a much shorter period. Their first win was 22 years ago and since then they have gained the honour on four other occasions having figured in four post-war finals including the present.

But in all probability it is the poignancy of local rivalry that will prove, as biggest factor in bringing public interest and enthusiasm in this afternoon's match. League performances are often at a discount in cup-ties and the lowly position of Dartford in the current Southern League table is by no means a sure guide to the outcome of to-day's game. Against Bromley in the semi-final, especially in the mid-week replay, Dartford adapted themselves much more readily to the conditions of a hard ground and a light ball than their opponents. On the other hand it has to be recognised that Gravesend and Northfleet mastered the strongly favoured Folkestone combination in a manner which left no doubt of their superiority. Thus spectators can look forward reasonably to an open and closely fought game this afternoon. With the impartiality due to the occasion I would only add that we can all hope for a good sporty exchange and may the better side win.

Right and below: The programme from the 1953 Kent Senior Cup final played at Gillingham in which Fleet beat their old rivals Dartford 2-1 in front of 8,876 supporters, Jack Winter and Bill McEwan scoring the goals.

DARTFORD   (WHITE SHIRTS)

1
NASH

2   3
NEWSTEAD   WALTON

5   6
CLARKE   WENHAM   PIPER

8   9   10   11
BAXHAM   GERMAN   URQUHART   HALL   PETERS

Referee: Mr. D. F. Rawlins
Linesman: Mr. L. J. Leckie
(Red Flag)
Mr. C. T. Holmes (Yellow Flag)

The teams are subject to alteration prior to the game and any changes will be announced.

11   10
HAIKES   WINTER   McEWAN   8   7
                                              HAWKINS   WAKEMAN

6   5   4
CARROLL   CLARK   LONGDON or JONES
                              CHAMBERS

3   2
DEEVEY   FLOCKHART or CHAMBERS

1
BLOWERS
GOULD

GRAVESEND & NORTHFLEET   (RED SHIRTS)

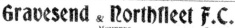

Gravesend & Northfleet F.C.

— MEMBERS — LIMITED

SOUTHERN LEAGUE   METROPOLITAN LEAGUE

Secretary-Manager—   CHAIRMAN—   Head Trainer—
W. J. MOSS   A. C. NORRIS-TELLING   J. OAKES

OFFICIAL PROGRAMME (Price 3d.)   No. 24

SOUTHERN LEAGUE

CHRISTMAS DAY, 25th DECEMBER 1953

Gravesend & Northfleet

v.

CHELMSFORD   № 875

Kick off 11.0 p.m.

RADIO and TELEVISION

SALES and SERVICE

A. J. HILL

6 STONE ST. GRAVESEND

TELEPHONE · · 449

Authorised Dealers for :—

ALBA, COSSOR, DECCA,
EVER-READY, FERGUSON,
H.M.V., INVICTA, K.B.,
MARCONI, PAM, PILOT,
R.G.D., REGENTONE, VIDOR,
etc.

K.B. MODEL KV35.
14-inch Tube.   16 valves.
DAYLIGHT VIEWING.
Cash Price: **61 gns.**
or **12/6** weekly

Cash or Hire Purchase Terms arranged
on any Model.

TELEVISION Installations completed
within 24 HOURS of placing order.

Left: Christmas Day football was a regular characteristic of football from Victorian times right up until 1959 when it finally ended. The custom was for a Christmas morning kick-off followed by a Boxing Day afternoon return match against the same opposition. Gravesend *v.* Dartford was the usual fixture but on this occasion Chelmsford provided the opposition for a game won 3–1 by the Fleet, who also won the following day, 4–3 at Writtle Street.

Opposite above: Gravesend was a popular destination for Football League teams and foreign sides, all of whom were eager to play under the new floodlighting system. Only Arsenal were quicker to have lights installed than the Fleet in London and the South East.

Below: The terrible floods of 31 January 1953 left the Thames Estuary in chaos. There was serious loss of life on the Essex side, notably on Canvey Island, but the Kent side was more fortunate. Amazingly, not a single fixture was lost at Stonebridge Road.

FLOODLIGHT FOOTBALL

MONDAY, 8th NOVEMBER, 1954

Gravesend & Northfleet
v.

Racing Club de Calais

Kick-off 7.30 p.m.

For value ..

Here's the very latest edition of the famous Bush T V 24, the most bought after 12" set that we handle. It's known as the T.V.24C. As well as those of the B.B.C. service, this model is capable of receiving the proposed (Tax Paid) alternative programmes within whatever proves to be the effective areas of the new transmitters.

54 GNS

Look to your BUSH dealer

Due to reliability and exceptional value, Bush Company are unable to meet the great demand, so order early to save disappointment.

BUSH MAIN DISTRIBUTORS

RAINBOW

PROGRAMME   PRICE THREEPENCE

FLOODLIGHT FOOTBALL

TUESDAY, 8th MARCH, 1955

Gravesend & Northfleet
v.

DUNKERQUOISE

Kick-off 7.30 p.m.

For value ..

Here's the very latest edition of the famous Bush T V 24, the most bought after 12" set that we handle. It's known as the T.V.24C. As well as those of the B.B.C. service, this model is capable of receiving the proposed (Tax Paid) alternative programmes within whatever proves to be the effective areas of the new transmitters.

54 GNS

Look to your BUSH dealer

Due to reliability and exceptional value, Bush Company are unable to meet the great demand, so order early to save disappointment.

BUSH MAIN DISTRIBUTORS

RAINBOW

PROGRAMME   PRICE THREEPENCE

GRAVESEND & NORTHFLEET F.C.
LTD.

Associate Members Football Association, Kent County F.A., Members Southern & Metrop. Bus. League.

DIRECTORS:
A. C. Norris-Telling, Chairman ; H. Merricks, Vice-Chairman ; A.E. Rutherell, Hon. Treasurer
F. Stevens, J.B.Rich, H.J. Town, S.C. Gray, J.R. Rowns.
Manager : J. Ross.   Secretary : D. Minter.
Hon. Medical Adviser : Dr. Maxwell Lamsac.
Colours : RED SHIRTS, WHITE COLLARS, WHITE SHORTS
Ground: STONEBRIDGE ROAD, NORTHFLEET. Tel.—Gravesend 3707.

No. 32.   OFFICIAL PROGRAMME (Price 3d.)

SATURDAY, 14th APRIL, 1956   No 099996
SOUTHERN LEAGUE

Gravesend & Northfleet
v.

MERTHYR

Kick-off 3 p.m.

The "Up-to-Date" TELEVISION

14in. FLAT SCREEN

TURRET TUNER FOR COMMERCIAL AND ALL B.B.C. PROGRAMMES

DAYLIGHT VIEWING

A. J. HILL

MODEL LVT30.

65 Gns. Cash or 10/6 Weekly

6 STONE STREET and 165 WINDMILL STREET GRAVESEND

Telephone:- Gravesend 449

ASK FOR

Truman's
"TRUBROWN"

(SPECIALLY BREWED BROWN ALE)

PERSONAL SUPERVISION

Smiths
CATERERS

Phone: Gravesend 588/9

DINNERS—WEDDINGS
DANCES—PARTIES

MAY WE QUOTE YOU?

TEAMS

GRAVESEND & NORTHFLEET UTD.—Red shirts, White shorts

HEATHCOTE

R   ENGLISH   DEEVEY   L

SMITH R.   CHAMBERS   GIBBONS

PARSONS   LOGIE   SCARTH   STEWART   POULTON

Referee:
Capt. C. Dennis

FURNITURE
Save 1/3 in the £—
Buy from the
RAINBOW
GRAVESEND

Linesmen:
R. Sharman
(Red Flag)

J. Silbery
(Yellow Flag)

DAVIES   REES   SLYME   TOFT   HOWARTH

WILLIAMSON   CARPENTER   JOHNSON

L   ANDERSON   LOWE   R

MERTHYR   JAMES

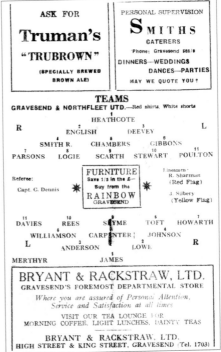

BRYANT & RACKSTRAW, LTD.
GRAVESEND'S FOREMOST DEPARTMENTAL STORE

Where you are assured of Personal Attention, Service and Satisfaction at all times

VISIT OUR TEA LOUNGE FOR
MORNING COFFEE, LIGHT LUNCHES, DAINTY TEAS

BRYANT & RACKSTRAW, LTD.
HIGH STREET & KING STREET, GRAVESEND (Tel. 1703)

Gravesend chalked up a record 8-1 victory over Merthyr in 1956 – a record equalled against Clacton in 1962 but never beaten. George Poulton led the way with a hat-trick while George Stewart bagged a brace and there were singles from Gordon Parsons, Jimmy Logie and Jimmy Scarth.

Frank Neary

Above: The floodlight trials of winter 1952 are watched by, from left to right, directors Frank Stevens (chairman 1965-1967), Arthur Norris-Telling (chairman 1952-1959 and 1964-1965), John Rigg, A.J. Stevens and Albert Rothwell.

Left: Frank Neary (1921-), a powerful centre forward who came to Northfleet as a thirty-four-year-old veteran in February 1955 and finished top scorer. He started the following season in the same way before moving on to Dartford before the end of November. His nine months at Stonebridge Road saw him score 22 goals in 26 matches – the best goal ratio of any Fleet player to play in more than twenty games. His playing career had seen him turn out for Queens Park Rangers, West Ham, Leyton Orient and Millwall before he joined the Fleet.

Right: Jackie Bridge (1932-). Born in Great Wakering, the stylish wing half and dead-eye penalty taker began his career at his local club, Southend, before moving to Gravesend in 1956. A lynchpin in the 1957/58 Southern League title-winning side, he eventually left for Sheppey in 1964 after 380 games and 39 goals, nearly all of them from the penalty spot. He later returned for a brief spell as manager at the start of the 1967/68 season.

Below: The 1955/56 side that finished twelfth in the Southern League. From left to right, back row: Charlie Poulton, Norman Lewis, Sam English, Peter Heathcote, Brian Moule, Sam Chambers. Front row: Lionel Smith, Jimmy Logie, Frank Neary, George Stewart, Jimmy Scarth.

Eddie Viles, United's latest capture, who was on Dartford's books before coming to North-fleet.

KEN JONES. GRAVESEND AND NORTHFLEET UTD.

GEORGE STEWART Gravesend and Northfleet Utd

A quartet of players in the popular cartoon form of the 1950s. Eddie Viles (far left) signed from Dartford in 1948, the inside forward playing 146 games and scoring 33 goals before moving on in 1952. George Brewster (left centre) was a prolific marksman who began with Bristol City before moving south to join the Fleet in 1951. He scored 62 goals in 92 games before a serious eye injury terminated his career in 1954, after a brave attempt at a comeback had failed. George was awarded a benefit match by the club because of the injury. Ken Jones (right centre) began at Southend before becoming one of Fleet's new full-time professionals in 1952. He played 55 games and scored once, later becoming a distinguished sports journalist with the *Daily Mirror*, *The Independent* and the BBC. George Stewart (far right) was another prolific marksman who scored 39 goals in just 62 games between 1954 and 1956.

THESE ENTRANCES AND GATES
WERE ERECTED IN 1957 BY
THE GRAVESEND AND NORTHFLEET
FOOTBALL SUPPORTERS ASSOCIATION
AS A MEMORIAL TO
MAJOR GEORGE STEPHEN SUNNUCKS
CHAIRMAN FROM 1946 TO 1955
AND PRESIDENT FROM 1955
UNTIL HIS DEATH ON
26th FEBRUARY 1957

The front entrance to the ground, rebuilt in 1957, was one of the most imposing in non-League football but sadly, like the ground itself, was allowed to deteriorate over the years. Many of the twelve turnstiles were put out of use and the canopy constantly hit by turning lorries was also taken down in 1998.

This page and overleaf: The contrasting fortunes of the FA Cup are portrayed in two sketches from the 1956/57 season: the high of crushing Bettshanger 7-1 and wiping away the bitter memory of a 3-1 defeat to the Colliers five years earlier – for former Fleet favourite Jim Deevey who played in the 1951/52 debacle it was a disaster as this time he was in the Colliers side – followed by the low of being dumped out by Sittingbourne in the next round (the third qualifying round) in front of a 5,000-plus crowd at the Bull ground by a 1-0 margin.

Right: Ron Walker (1931-). Signed from Sittingbourne in 1956, this inside forward made an immediate impact, top-scoring with 17 goals in 1956/57, but was unable to reproduce that form the following season and left in 1958 having scored a respectable 25 goals from 54 games.

Below: Jimmy Logie explains to his teammates how they will wipe the floor with the opposition in the 1957/58 season. The players at the pre-season training session are, from left to right: Jimmy Logie, Derek Styles, Mick Martin, Tom Tilston, Eddie Lyons, Eric Day, Harry MacDonald and Bob Thomas. Logie was proved right as Fleet went on to win the Southern League title.

Above left: Jimmy Scarth (1926-2000). North Shields-born Jimmy scored 86 goals in 248 matches for Fleet between 1955 and 1960. A right-winger or centre forward, he also played for Tottenham and Gillingham, once scoring a hat-trick in three minutes with the latter – a record only recently beaten.

Above right: Sam Chambers (1927-) was one of the great Fleet stalwarts and the record appearance holder until overhauled by Ken Burrett in the 1980s. He began after the war with Gravesend United and switched to the newly formed Fleet when they began. Sam played at centre half or full-back, the highlight of his Fleet career coming when he skippered the 1952/53 side to the Kent Senior Cup. He received two benefit games in a Fleet career that spanned 1946-1961. In all he played 495 first-team games scoring 12 goals, and also a considerable number of reserve-team games later in his career. Sam was also a notable local village cricketer, playing well into middle age.

Opposite above, left: Dartford-born Eric Day (1921-). After war service in the Commandos he joined Southampton in 1946, playing 398 games on the right wing between 1946 and 1957 and scoring 145 goals. He was a key signing for the Fleet in 1957 and switched to centre forward with great effect, scoring 29 goals in the Southern League title-winning side. He struggled with injury and decided to retire at the end of the 1958/59 season with an excellent record of 44 goals from 55 games.

Eric Day

Above right: Jimmy Robertson (1929-). The twinkle-toed Scotsman began his career at Dunipace Thistle before moving to Arsenal in 1951. After two seasons in which he was always a fringe player on the left wing, he moved to Brentford (1953-1955) and then on to Fleet after manager Lionel Smith remembered his talented former teammate. Jimmy made his debut at the start of the 1956/57 season and went on to be a vital member of the championship side of 1957/58. He had made 207 appearances and scored 37 goals when his career came to a sudden end when he suffered a broken leg at Stonebridge Road whilst playing against Folkestone in February 1961 at a time when he was still at the top of his game.

Right: Joe Thompson (1927-1996), another of Fleet's 1957/58 championship-winning team. Born in Seaham, he moved south and began his senior career at Luton before moving on to Shrewsbury. He then moved south again, playing for Hastings, from whom he joined the Fleet in 1956, making 79 appearances in three seasons and scoring 4 goals.

Arthur Shaw (1924-). Born in Limehouse, Arthur was a larger-than-life character who skippered the Fleet's championship side of 1957/58 from right half. He had started at Hayes before being snapped up by Brentford. He made the move to Arsenal in 1949 where he spent five years without ever grabbing a regular place and moved onto Watford before his old teammate Lionel Smith added him to his growing list of ex-Arsenal players at Gravesend in 1956. He made 124 appearances and scored 9 goals for the club before retiring at the end of 1958/59 season.

Sam English. This craggy Scot was born in Dundee and, after playing for Arbroath and Albion Rovers, played for his home-town team Dundee United at centre half or full-back. Sam moved south in 1954 and considerably strengthened a wobbly Fleet defence. Another member of the 1957/58 championship side, he played 201 games for the club before retiring in 1961 after a well-earned and successful benefit. He died in 1987.

Bob Thomas (1919-1990). Born in Stepney, the free-scoring inside forward was top marksman in the 1957/58 title-winning team – just as he had been the previous season when he had picked up a winners' medal with Kettering, along with fellow Fleetman Harry MacDonald. Bob had played for Brentford, Plymouth, Fulham, Crystal Palace and Kettering before joining Fleet. At the end of the 1958/59 season, having scored 82 goals in 104 games, he was allowed to move on to Clacton, whom he inspired to promotion into the Southern League Premier Division.

Lionel Smith (1920-1980). Born in Mexborough, Yorkshire, Lionel joined Arsenal from Denaby in 1939, playing 162 games for the Gunners and winning both a Football League Championship and an FA Cup as well as earning several England international caps at full-back in a career considerably reduced by war. He moved on to Watford and then joined Fleet as player-manager in January 1955. A persistent knee injury restricted him to just 12 appearances before retirement allowed him to concentrate on his managerial role. His strong connections in the game enabled him to sign many quality players and Fleet swept to the Southern League title in 1957/58. Sadly, at the end of the 1959/60 season he decided against renewing his contract and moved into the licensing trade, never to manage a football team again.

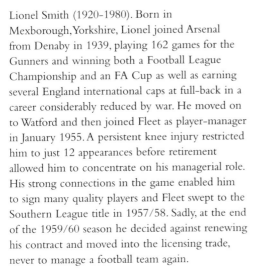

Peter Heathcote (1932-). The Leicester-born goalkeeper moved to Gravesend in 1955 after several seasons at Southend and quickly made the goalkeeper's role his own, culminating in some fine displays in the 1957/58 championship side. In all, he made 275 appearances before moving to Dartford in 1960.

Wednesday 30 April 1958 was a red-letter day for the club as Hastings were beaten in front of 6,269 by a 3-1 margin to clinch the Southern League title for the first and only time. Jimmy Scarth bagged two and Bob Thomas the other.

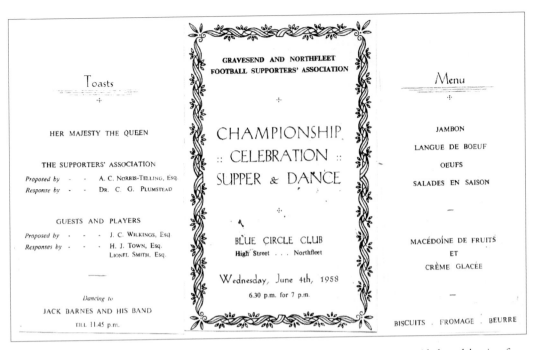

Toasts
.:.

HER MAJESTY THE QUEEN

THE SUPPORTERS' ASSOCIATION
Proposed by   -   -   A. C. Norris-Telling, Esq.
Response by   -   -   Dr. C. G. Plumstead

GUESTS AND PLAYERS
Proposed by   -   -   -   J. C. Wilkings, Esq
Responses by   -   -   -   H. J. Town, Esq.
                              Lionel Smith, Esq.

——

Dancing to
JACK BARNES AND HIS BAND
Till 11.45 p.m.

GRAVESEND AND NORTHFLEET
FOOTBALL SUPPORTERS' ASSOCIATION

.:.

CHAMPIONSHIP
:: CELEBRATION ::
SUPPER & DANCE

.:.

BLUE CIRCLE CLUB
High Street . . . Northfleet

Wednesday, June 4th, 1958
6.30 p.m. for 7 p.m.

Menu
.:.

JAMBON
LANGUE DE BOEUF
OEUFS
SALADES EN SAISON

—

MACÉDOINE DE FRUITS
ET
CRÈME GLACÉE

—

BISCUITS . FROMAGE . BEURRE

Party time following the championship success as the Supporters' Association provided a celebration for players, supporters and officials.

Champions at last! How the cartoonist Mickey Durling saw the success. Clockwise from bottom left are Joe Thompson, Eric Day, Charlie Carson, Harry MacDonald, Arthur Shaw, Jimmy Logie, Bob Thomas; Jackie Bridge and Jimmy Robertson shaking hands; Lionel Smith, Sam English, Peter Heathcote; Arthur Norris Telling and Albert Rothwell shaking hands.

Harry MacDonald (1926-2004). Born in Salford, this stylish left-back moved south to Crystal Palace in 1950 from Ashton United before moving on to Kettering in 1955. Having won a Southern League title with the Poppies in 1956/57, he then did likewise with the Fleet and was the only player who appeared in both that success and the cup giant-killing side of 1962/63. Harry retired at the end of 1963/64 and had a very successful benefit game as befitted a highly popular and loyal player who clocked up 308 appearances but never scored a goal.

Jimmy Logie

Jimmy Logie (1919-1984). The wee Scot – just 5ft 4in – was born in Edinburgh and began with Lochore Welfare before moving to Arsenal just three months before war broke out in 1939. He eventually made 296 appearances and scored 68 goals for the Gunners, winning both League and FA Cup medals and a single Scotland cap. His signing for Gravesend in January 1955 was a major coup as a string of clubs had chased his signature and Fleet were rock bottom of the Southern League at the time. Thirty-five at the time, it looked likely to be a short-term deal, but Logie played for five seasons and helped the club go from bottom to top before retiring in December 1959 to take over the Greyhound, Stoke Newington. He had played 217 games and scored 47 goals and remains probably the best player to don a Fleet shirt.

Arguably the best side to ever put on the Fleet's red shirt and certainly the most entertaining, the 1957/58 championship side proved once again that stability rather than constant changes makes for a successful side. In a 42-match league programme only nineteen players were used, and seven of those made only single-figure appearances, with eleven of the team making 30 appearances or more. All the regulars are included in this photo except that the unlucky Sam Chambers made only five appearances before injury kept him out and he was replaced by Sam English. From left to right, back row: Lionel Smith (manager), Charlie Carson, Arthur Shaw (captain), Jackie Bridge, Peter Heathcote, Sam Chambers, Joe Thompson, Harry MacDonald, Dave Thomas (trainer). Front row: Jimmy Scarth, Jimmy Logie, Eric Day, Bob Thomas, Jimmy Robertson.

The 1959/60 side line up before the FA Cup fourth qualifying round tie with Ashford. Disappointment was waiting as, for the third year running, they fell at the final hurdle before the competition proper, losing 2-1. From left to right, back row: Jimmy Robertson, Harry MacDonald, Sam English, Jackie Bridge, Norman Coe, Charlie Carson, Jimmy Fletcher, Dave Thomas (trainer). Front row: Jimmy Scarth, Jimmy Logie, Alan Brown, Kevin Baron, Johnny Simmonds.

Kevin Baron

Kevin Baron (1926-1991). Born in Preston, Kevin played 140 games for Liverpool including a runners-up medal in the 1950 FA Cup final before moving on to Southend and Northampton. He signed for Gravesend in 1959 and was heralded as a major signing to help Fleet compete in the enlarged Southern League, now with promotion and relegation, but he was never able to produce his best at inside forward in an injury-plagued season. He moved briefly back into the Football League with Aldershot before ending his career at Wisbech.

GOODBYE Jimmy and GOOD LUCK

FORMER ARSENAL STAR AND SCOTTISH INTERNATIONAL— JIMMY LOGIE IS HANGING UP HIS BOOTS FOR GOOD

'Goodbye Jimmy and good luck' was the perfect caption as the wee maestro decided that at forty his time was up, his weary limbs protesting more and more after each match in a season in which he was always targeted by the opposition as one of the main men to stop – one way or another. But he had one final trick up his sleeve for his farewell game against Wisbech Town at Stonebridge Road on 5 December 1959, putting in a five-star show as the Fenmen were demolished 7-1 with Logie scoring one of the goals. At this stage of the season Fleet were well placed in the very first season of the Southern League Premier Division but without Logie pulling the strings the club was like a ship without an anchor and only just avoided relegation after going into freefall.

five

Giant-killing, Relegation and Money Troubles 1960-1969

Ron Humpston (1923-) was a Derby-born goalkeeper who played in goal for Portsmouth and Huddersfield before moving abroad to coach. He was appointed manager of Gravesend in 1960 with the difficult task of following the popular and successful Lionel Smith. Ron's bold policy was to give youth its chance, and whilst this was highly creditable and initially successful, the team gradually faded and only just avoided relegation on goal average. Matters failed to improve during the early months of the 1961/62 season and he was sacked in November 1961.

Roy Dwight (1933-2002). This Erith-born right-winger began at Fulham and moved on to Nottingham Forest in 1957, where he had a bittersweet career, perfectly encapsulated by his most famous game, the 1959 FA Cup final. In that match he scored the first goal for Forest but then broke his leg and had his winners' medal – after Forest beat Luton 2-1 – presented to him in a hospital bed. He never quite recovered his sharpness and, living in north Kent, the move to Gravesend in 1961 was perfect for him. He quickly settled and less than a year later he was sold to Coventry City, where his former teammate Jimmy Hill was now making a name for himself as a manager, for £2,000. For Fleet he played at centre forward, scoring 14 goals in 37 matches. Roy later managed Tooting and Dartford and was stadium manager at Crayford dog track but in later years his achievements in football tended to be forgotten as he was instead known for being the cousin of Reg Dwight (a.k.a. Elton John).

An improvised assault course was erected in the club car park by new manager Ron Humpston for preseason training in 1960 to help fitness. Leading the way are reserve-team players Brian Homersham, Ivan Clarke and John Tank.

Above left: Reg Edmonds (1940-) was signed from Fulham in 1960 and top-scored from the centre forward or inside right position in a struggling 1960/61 team. He left after one season to join the police force. He had scored 21 goals in 46 matches.

Above right: Mickey Cross (1940-). Another signing from Fulham in 1960 and another rare success in a poor season, playing on the right wing. After two seasons he moved on but returned again in 1963/64, by which time he had dropped into midfield. In all, he made 101 appearances, scoring 20 goals.

GILLINGHAM FOOTBALL CLUB Co., LTD.
Priestfield Stadium   Gillingham

A MESSAGE TO OUR HOSTS

The Board of Directors of Gillingham F.C. take this opportunity of expressing their grateful thanks to the Board of Gravesend & Northfleet F.C. for the help and co-operation given to us in this emergency.
We in our turn, will do everything to enhance this good relationship. We welcome Wrexham F.C. Directors and Staff to Gravesend, and trust the game on this good ground will be worthy of two F.L. clubs.

CHAIRMAN & DIRECTORS.
GILLINGHAM F.C.

NEXT HOME MATCHES

Easter Monday, April 3rd SOUTHPORT   K.O. 3.00 p.m.
Wednesday, April 5th DOVER   K.O. 3.00 p.m.
Saturday, April 8th ROCHDALE   K.O. 3.00 p.m.
Saturday, April 15th BETTESHANGER   K.O. 3.00 p.m.

DRINK
MEUX'S
TREBLE GOLD
ALWAYS OBTAINABLE IN TIP-TOP CONDITION

GILLINGHAM FOOTBALL CLUB
v
WREXHAM
FOOTBALL LEAGUE DIVISION 4
Saturday, March 25th, 1961
K.O. 3.00 p.m.

programme 3d.

Ernie Walley

Above left: On 25 March 1961, for the first and only time, the Football League came to Stonebridge Road when Gillingham met Wrexham in a Fourth Division game won by the Welsh side 3-0. The reason the game was played at Northfleet was the closing of Priestfield by the FA following a pitch invasion by spectators in which the referee was knocked to the ground after the Gills had lost to Oldham Athletic. Thirty-nine years later the Gills were able to return the favour when the FA Cup first round game between Gravesend and Notts County was transferred to Priestfield after constant postponements because of waterlogging.

Above right: Ernie Walley (1933-) was born in Caernarfon and signed for Tottenham in 1951 but managed only six appearances in five years. The stylish wing half moved to Middlesbrough and then on to Guildford City, from whom he joined the Fleet in November 1961. Ernie featured strongly in the FA Cup giant-killing side of 1962/63 and made 77 appearances for the club, scoring 6 goals, before moving to Stevenage at the end of the 1962/63 season.

Boxing Day 1962 was not one to remember. It was bad enough that the Southern League had sent them to Worcester but much worse came when the first snowfalls of what was to be a bitter winter turned the game into a farce. Even worse, relegation looked even more likely after this 3-1 defeat. In this picture Tony Cottrill's shot is blocked by Tony Newcombe while Johny Sanchez looks on. It was well past midnight when the team arrived home in Kent.

The first sign that perhaps a good cup run was on the way was the 5-0 demolition of unbeaten Erith & Belverdere on 6 October 1962.

STAN'S BACK
"ONLY MANAGING"

1 MAY AVENUE,
NORTHFLEET,
GRAVESEND, KENT.

ALDOUS BROS.

PORTABLE BUILDINGS   FENCING AND TIMBER

GRAVESEND & NORTHFLEET F.C.
LIMITED

Associate Members Football Association, Kent County F.A.
Members Southern League and Metropolitan League
Directors:
H. Morrison, Chairman; A. C. Norris-Telling, Vice-Chairman; A. E. Rothwell
F. Stevens, H. J. Town, S. G. Gray
Secretary: G. E. Fooks. Hon. Treasurer: A. E. Rothwell
Manager: W. H. C. Lane
Ground: Stonebridge Road, Northfleet. Tel.—Gravesend 3790
Colours: Red Shirts, White Collars, White Shorts

No. 4   OFFICIAL PROGRAMME
F.A. CUP—1st Round Qualifying   N° 926
SATURDAY, SEPTEMBER 8, 1962

Gravesend & Northfleet
v.
Chatham
Kick-off 3 p.m.

RAINBOW
GRAVESEND   Phone 2919

Agents for: G.E.C.,
Sole Agents for BUSH
FERGUSON, PYE,
EKCO, ULTRA,
PHILIPS

BUSH
With
pre-selection
station
change

SUPPLIED ON CASH OR EASY TERMS

STAN'S BACK
"ONLY MANAGING"

1 MAY AVENUE,
NORTHFLEET,
GRAVESEND, KENT.

ALDOUS BROS.

PORTABLE BUILDINGS   FENCING AND TIMBER

GRAVESEND & NORTHFLEET F.C.
LIMITED

Associate Members Football Association, Kent County F.A.
Members Southern League and Metropolitan League
Directors:
H. Morrison, Chairman; A. C. Norris-Telling, Vice-Chairman; A. E. Rothwell
F. Stevens, H. J. Town, S. G. Gray
Secretary: G. E. Fooks. Hon. Treasurer: A. E. Rothwell
Manager: W. H. C. Lane
Ground: Stonebridge Road, Northfleet. Tel.—Gravesend 3790
Colours: Red Shirts, White Collars, White Shorts

No. 21   OFFICIAL PROGRAMME
F.A. CUP—4th Round Proper

Gravesend & Northfleet
v.
Sunderland
Kick-off 7.30 p.m.

RAINBOW
GRAVESEND   Phone 2919

Agents for: G.E.C.,
Sole Agents for BUSH
FERGUSON, PYE,
EKCO, ULTRA,
PHILIPS

BUSH
With

SUPPLIED ON CASH OR EASY TERMS

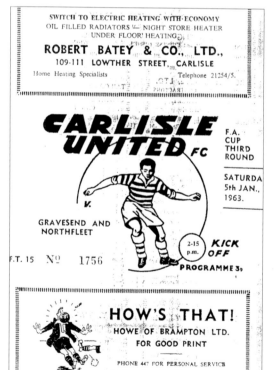

SWITCH TO ELECTRIC HEATING WITH ECONOMY
OIL FILLED RADIATORS — NIGHT STORE HEATER
UNDER FLOOR HEATING

ROBERT BATEY & CO., LTD.,
109-111 LOWTHER STREET, CARLISLE
Home Heating Specialists   Telephone 21254/5.

CARLISLE UNITED FC
v.
GRAVESEND AND
NORTHFLEET

F.A.
CUP
THIRD
ROUND

SATURDAY
5th JAN.,
1963.

2-15
p.m.   KICK
OFF

F.T. 15   N° 1756   PROGRAMME 3d

HOW'S THAT!
HOWE OF BRAMPTON LTD.
FOR GOOD PRINT
PHONE 447 FOR PERSONAL SERVICE

SEASON 1962-63   OFFICIAL PROGRAMME
4d

SUNDERLAND
ASS'N FOOTBALL CLUB LTD · ROKER PARK

F.A. CUP WINNERS — 1937
DIV. 1 LEAGUE CHAMPIONS
1891-92   1892-93   1894-95
1901-02   1912-13   1935-36

No. 31

F.A. CUP—4th ROUND
REPLAY

Sunderland
v.
Gravesend & Northfleet

Kick-off 7-15 p.m.

Above: The 3-1 second-round victory over Wycombe Wanderers on 24 November 1962 as seen by Micky Durling.

Opposite page, above left: The record-breaking FA Cup run began on 8 September 1962 with a less-than-convincing 2-1 win over Chatham Town and ended five months and ten days later at Sunderland on 18 February 1963. This was the longest time any club had been involved in the competition in its near-100-year history and, although Blyth Spartans exactly equalled the achievement with their great run of 1977/78, the record has never been beaten in the 125 years of the FA Cup.

Opposite page, above right and below: Three more programmes from that great cup run. The Carlisle match due to take place on 5 January was eventually staged, after five postponements, on 29 January and it can be noted that neither of the Gravesend *v.* Sunderland matches had a scheduled date on the programme because cancellations were expected due to the constant weather problems. As it turned out, this happened with the first game but not the replay.

The great marathon cup run finally came off the rails at an icy Roker Park against Sunderland in a fourth-round replay on 18 February 1963. Centre half Tony Newcombe, the club's outstanding defender of the '60s, helps foil another Sunderland attack.

Everybody except goalkeeper Peter Reader is having trouble staying on his feet. The Fleet players are Harry McDonald (far left) and Tony Newcombe (far right).

Fleet's best players on the night, goalkeeper Peter Reader and centre half Tony Newcombe, combine to
foil the Sunderland attack in the 5-2 defeat. Bob McNicol and Bob Finch fail to stop Irish international
Johnny Crossan putting Sunderland 4-0 up. The game would be eventful for McNicol who scored one
of Fleet's goals and later got sent off.

Bob McNicol (1933-1980). Dumbarton-born
Bob was one of the Fleet's giant-killing heroes
of the 1962/63 season. He was a rugged full-
back who had played more than 200 Football
League games for Accrington Stanley and
Brighton, from whom he joined Fleet as one of
a new breed of full-time players in 1962. In an
eventful cup run he scored the winner to put
Exeter out in the first round and also scored at
Sunderland before being sent off. He left for
Carlisle in October 1963 after playing 62 games
and scoring 4 goals for the club. He was killed
in a plane crash in Tenerife in 1980.

69

Bobby Cameron (1932-). This Greenock-born inside forward was another cup hero of 1962/63. His stylish play at Port Glasgow tempted Queens Park Rangers to bring him south and he made 256 appearances between 1950 and 1958 before moving on to Leeds United. Bobby joined the Fleet in 1962 as one of several full-time players. A troublesome knee injury restricted him to 41 appearances and 7 goals before he moved back into the Football League briefly with Southend in October 1963. He later emigrated to Australia, where he still lives.

Chester-born Alan Humphreys (1939-) was a goalkeeper who seemed destined for the top when playing 32 times for Shrewsbury as a teenager before moving on to Leeds and earning England Under-23 caps, but after two years at Leeds, in which period injuries restricted him to just 40 appearances, he moved south to join Gravesend as a full-timer. Again injury reduced his appearances and, after playing in all the FA Cup games of 1962, the games at Carlisle and Sunderland saw his deputy Peter Reader step into the breech. In all, he played 44 times for the club before getting back into the Football League and playing more than 100 times for Mansfield and Chesterfield, showing what a good goalkeeper he was.

Brian Skingley (1937-1999). Born in Romford, Brian played originally at full-back, signing for Bristol Rovers and then moving on to Crystal Palace without breaking through to claim a regular spot at either club. His boisterous style led him to also playing at centre forward – a position he filled perfectly at Stonebridge Road after signing in November 1962. He made himself an instant hit with the fans by scoring a hat-trick in only his second match and then scoring twice against Wycombe to put Fleet through to the third round of the FA Cup. He then laid on the winner for Tony Sitford at Carlisle and scored the goal that saw Stonebridge Road erupt against Sunderland, a game in which he sustained an injury that saw him miss the replay at a time when he was at the peak of his career. He left at the end of the season but returned briefly in 1968/69. In all, he made 45 appearances and scored 12 goals for the club.

Barry Fry (1945-). Born in Bedford, this schoolboy international appeared to have a great career ahead of him and joined Manchester United, but was never able to establish himself. After short, equally unsuccessful spells at Bolton and Luton he found himself at Stonebridge Road in 1966. He quickly found form and when Walter Rickett left to become assistant manager at Leyton Orient he quickly returned to bring Fry with him. Fry had played just 20 matches and scored 2 goals for the Fleet from midfield. He later became much better known as a manager at Barnet, Maidstone, Southend, Birmingham and Peterborough.

Another Micky Durling drawing, this time of the Gravesend *v.* Sunderland game which attracted a ground-record 12,032 to Stonebridge Road on 12 February 1963 to see a 1-1 draw in the fourth round.

Wally Bellett (1933-). Stratford born Wally – 'Belly Wallett' to Fleet fans – was an England Youth international full-back who never quite fulfilled his potential. He moved around the country after starting at Chelsea, with stays at Plymouth, Chester, Wrexham and Tranmere, from whom he signed for Northfleet in 1964. He totalled 78 appearances and scored a single goal in his two seasons with the club.

Walter Rickett (1917-1991) was a Sheffield-born winger whose playing career highlight was playing for Blackpool on the opposite wing to Stanley Matthews in the 1948 FA Cup final, which Manchester United won 4-2. Walter later played for both Sheffield clubs, Rotherham and Halifax before moving to Kent, where he managed both Ramsgate and Sittingbourne before taking over at Gravesend in 1963. He even made a single Southern League appearance and, at forty-six, remains the oldest player to turn out for Fleet. He left the club in 1966 after three years of struggle to become assistant manager of Leyton Orient.

Walter Rickett

Left: Brothers Brian (left) and John Roche line up before the 1964/65 season. They had contrasting fortunes with Brian playing only four times on the left wing without scoring, while inside forward John top-scored in his single season with the club, netting 10 goals in 42 games. He had earlier played for Millwall, Crystal Palace and Margate. He later made further history when his son, also John, played for Fleet 16 times during the 1986/87 season. They were the first of three father and son duos to play for the club; Pip and Danny Jeffrey and Bob and Danny Glozier later also achieved this feat.

Below: Gravesend were desperately unlucky to lose 1-0 at Brentford in the second round of the FA Cup on 7 December 1963. Here Mike Wilkins tries his luck at goal watched by Harry Easton, a survivor of the great cup run of the previous season. Mel Scott takes evasive action for the Bees.

Above: Two seasons on and Fleet are again on FA Cup duty, this time in a first-round game at Plough Lane which Wimbledon won 4-1. Peter Chamberlain (out of picture) fires the ball home from a half-cleared corner to reduce the score to 2-1.

Right: Alan Crudace was a great servant of the club through some pretty rough times. The South Shields-born defender signed from Hastings in 1965 and remained until 1973 amassing 394 games and scoring 8 goals before returning to his home-town club.

Jim Towers (1933-). Born in Shepherds Bush, 'Big Jim' scored nearly 200 Football League goals for Brentford, Queens Park Rangers, Millwall, Gillingham and Aldershot and scored five in a game against Gravesend & Northfleet while playing for Romford, from whom Fleet signed him in 1965. Although past his best, his thunderous shooting over the next two seasons made him a great crowd favourite as he scored 48 goals in 87 matches in a struggling team. Big Jim retired early in the 1967/68 season as injuries took their toll.

George Waites (1938-2000) was a Stepney-born inside forward who had played for Leyton Orient, Norwich and Brighton before joining Fleet in 1965. He scored 21 goals in 109 games in a three-year stay in which, along with Jim Towers, he was a mainstay of the forward line.

Right: Phil Brooman was a London-born goalkeeper who joined the Fleet from Margate and made his debut in 1965, making 73 appearances in a two-year stay in which he proved himself a highly capable goalkeeper and became popular with the crowd. He left for Canterbury City in 1967.

Below: Jim Towers threatens the Banbury goal during a 1966/67 clash that was typical of his stay. He scored twice but Banbury made the most of defensive lapses to win 4-2. The days of a pre-terrace Swanscombe end can be clearly seen in the background.

Johnny Dick

Left: John Dick (1930-2000). This Glasgow-born inside forward had an excellent career with West Ham, where he played 326 games and scored 153 goals between 1953 and 1962, and then played 72 games and scored 44 times for Brentford. Sadly, on signing for Fleet his career was dogged by injury. He took over from the departing manager Walter Rickett in October 1966 with a job description of coach rather than manager but, with black financial clouds again forming, his task was hopeless and he departed at the end of the season having played just 10 games and scored 3 goals.

Below: Rock-bottom Gravesend caused a major upset in the quarter-finals of the Kent Senior Cup by beating Ramsgate 4-2. Two months earlier in a Southern League game at the same venue the high-riding Rams had dispatched Fleet 6-0. Pictured is Alan Crudace (2) climbing highest to clear a Ramsgate attack, watched by Gordon Gilham (4). Kent Senior Cup games were still played on Saturdays in the 1960s.

Former Ashford and Wimbledon goalkeeper Eddie McAlpine signed for Fleet in 1967 and became the third manager of the season at a time when the club were at their lowest ebb. He did improve matters slightly in his player-manager role but broke his leg playing against Corby in 1968 and was sacked a month later.

Alf Ackerman (1929-1988). South African-born Alf had an impressive goal tally in his playing career as a centre forward with Clyde, Norwich, Hull, Derby, Carlisle and Millwall. He began his managerial career with Dartford and was surprisingly sacked after four relatively successful seasons. After a break he was persuaded back into the game by his fellow newsagent, Fleet chairman Vic Troke, and as manager helped put Fleet back on the road to success after the grim days of the mid and late 1960s, earning promotion back to the Southern League Premier Division. He eventually left in March 1974 having groomed his assistant Tony Sitford to take over. Alf returned to South Africa and died there in 1988.

Right: Colin Murphy played at full-back for the best part of three seasons between 1968 and 1971, making 80 appearances for the Fleet and helping them gain promotion to the Southern League Premier Division in 1970/71. It was as a coach and manager that he had his greatest success, managing Lincoln, Derby and Stockport. He is currently assistant manager at Hull City.

Opposite: Chatham-born Alan Lillis was a rock-solid defender signed from Dartford who helped inspire Fleet to promotion back to the Southern League Premier Division in 1971. His two seasons, 1969/70 and 1970/71, yielded 91 appearances and 13 goals before he moved on to Maidstone United.

Roy Hodgson

Roy Hodgson was a contemporary of Murphy at Northfleet, playing in midfield. He made 59 appearances between 1969 and 1971 but then moved into coaching, at which he excelled, later managed in various countries and also at Blackburn Rovers. He just failed in his bid to become the only English manager at the 2006 World Cup finals when his Kazakstan side were beaten in the play-offs.

Stan Aldous

Stan Aldous (1923-1995) was Northfleet-born and one of the most successful players to come from the area. A solid, no-nonsense centre half, he began his career at Bromley with brother Gilbert before moving back to his home-town club at the tail end of the 1947/48 season. His fine displays were a major factor in the club winning their first honour in 1948/49 with the Kent Senior Cup success over Gillingham. He moved on to Leyton Orient in 1950 and played 302 games for them, including skippering the side to the Third Division (South) title and promotion. After a spell at Headington he went into business owning a factory in Northfleet and became Fleet manager (unpaid) in 1967/68. The club were in desperate financial trouble and the team were rock bottom of the Southern League – and even Stan couldn't turn this situation around. He even had to play himself briefly, bringing his overall tally of games for the club to 111, with 3 goals.

six

On the Up
1970-1979

Tony Nicholas

Above: A great start to the new decade as promotion back to the Southern League Premier Division is achieved by the 1970/71 side, who finished third.

Left: West Ham-born Tony Nicholas (1938-2005) was a free-scoring forward who was reaching the end of his career when he joined Gravesend from Dartford in November 1971. In a struggling team destined for relegation he managed to top-score, and moved to Folkestone in January 1973 having scored 19 goals in 43 matches for Fleet. He had begun his career at Chelsea and moved on to play for Brighton, Leyton Orient, Cambridge United and Chelmsford.

Opposite below: The 1974/75 season brought great success, the club winning the Southern League South with only two defeats all season. Pictured presenting a watch to manager Tony Sitford for all his efforts ahead of the last game of the season are, from left to right, back row: Pip Jeffrey, Mickey Angel, Johnny Thurgood, Dave Bostock, Phil Debnam, Colin Norman, John Cowan, Kenny Burrett. Front row: Brian Woolfe, Ken Pearce, Tony Weston, Tony Sitford, Colin Blaber and Ray Hutchins.

Above: The first match of the 1973/74 season saw Fleet entertain Waterlooville and record a comfortable 3-0 win. Brian Woolfe wins this heading duel with Dave Bostock backing him up. The other two Fleet players shown are Peter Allwright (left) and Dave Laurie (right). Despite the bright start, Fleet could only finish tenth to the visitors third.

'My best moment of 17 years in football', was how Manager Tony Sitford described the presentation to him of a watch by the 'Fleet players before the final game of the season. From left to right: Back row, Pip Jeffrey, Mickey Angel, Johnny Thurgood, Dave Bostock, Phil Debnam, Colin Norman, John Cowen, Kenny Burrett. Front row, Brian Woolfe, Les Hall, Ken Pearce, Tony Weston, 'The Boss' Tony Sitford, Colin Blaber, Ray Hutchins.

Champions! After beating Metropolitan Police 3-0 in the final game of the season the team are awarded their trophies amid much celebration. From left to right: John Cowan, Dave Bostock, Brian Woolfe (partly obscured), Tony Sitford, Ray Hutchins, Colin Norman (partly obscured), Tony Weston, Phil Debnam and Ken Pearce.

Above left: Tommy Baldwin (1945-) was a Gateshead-born forward who began at Arsenal before moving across London to Chelsea, where his eventful stay between 1966 and 1974 gained him both FA Cup and European Cup-Winners' Cup medals. He later moved on to Millwall before trying his luck with the Fleet in August 1976. Sadly, injuries restricted him to just 7 appearances for the club, although to his credit he battled back to fitness later and returned to the Football League with Brentford.

Above right: Andy Woon (1952-). This Bognor Regis-born centre forward began his career at his home-town club and made a big impact as a teenage goalscorer. He was snapped up by Brentford, for whom he scored 12 times in 50 games. He then moved to Maidstone before signing for the Fleet in 1976. A member of the Southern League Cup-winning side, he was a useful foil for wide men Steve Brown and Brian Woolfe, scoring 49 goals in 145 outings before returning to Maidstone in 1979.

Above left: Edmonton-born Lee Smelt (1958-) began his career at Colchester and moved on to Margate, from whom Tony Sitford snapped him up in September 1976. He went on to become perhaps Gravesend's greatest goalkeeper. Only eighteen when he began his Fleet career, he made 208 appearances for the club, featuring in the Southern League Cup-winning side and the team that made the Alliance Premier League. Lee moved to Nottingham Forest for £15,000 and then on to Cardiff, Halifax and Peterborough before returning to Kent football with Welling and Margate, whom he later managed.

Above right: Steve Brown makes the vital breakthrough in extra time to give Gravesend the lead against Weymouth in the 1977/78 Southern League Cup final. The first leg in Dorset had ended goalless and another ninety minutes at Stonebridge Road had done likewise. When Brian Woolfe headed a second the cup was Fleet's for the first time.

The outstanding side of 1977/78. From left to right, back row: Brian Hawkes, John Hawker, David Hockley, Jack Bennett, Fred Wilmshurst, Trevor Bonneywell (all directors). Middle row: Danny Keenan (trainer), Andy Woon, Dave Bostock, Ken Burrett, Lee Smelt, Bob Dudman, Graham Byford, Colin Priestley. Front row: Alan Fagan, Steve Brown, Geoff Idle, Roger Easterby (chairman), George Jacks, Tony Sitford (manager), Brian Woolfe, Norman Fusco, Bob Finch.

Above left: Bob Glozier raises the cup in front of delighted Fleet fans.

Above right: Phil Stonebridge was a vital signing from Maidstone to help ensure Gravesend qualified for the newly formed Alliance Premier League. He top-scored in each of his three seasons with the club (1978-1981), in all scoring 46 goals in 151 appearances before moving on to Tonbridge.

Left: Alan Hart (1956-). This Woolwich-born midfielder began as an apprentice at Charlton and moved onto Millwall, making a handful of Football League games for both clubs before joining Dulwich Hamlet. He joined the Fleet in time for the club's first season in the Alliance League in 1979 and soon settled down, making a midfield berth his own. He played through to the end of 1984/85, by which time he had racked up 214 appearances and 25 goals.

Gravesend proudly line up with the Southern League Cup at the start of the 1978/79 season. From left to right, back row: Trevor Bonneywell, John Keirs, Keith Down, Peter Osborne, John Cowen, Lee Smelt, David Hockley, Brian Hawkes, Jack Bennett (all directors). Middle row: Ken Burrett, Colin Blaber (trainer), Micky Johnson, Kevin Wallis, Gary Aldous, Chris Keys, Bob Dudman, Andy Woon, Bob Wiles (reserve trainer). Front row: Steve Brown, Geoff Idle, Bob Glozier, Roger Easterby (chairman), Dave Sargent, Tony Sitford (manager), Brian Woolfe, Len Tomkins, Phil Stonebridge.

Three main reasons for the club's success in the late 1970s. Chairman Roger Easterby (left) was the driving force, keeping the club in the public eye and pushing them on to challenge Maidstone and Dartford as the premier Kent club. He was in the chair between 1974 and 1982 before a financial crisis saw him depart soon after the club's relegation from the Alliance League. George Jacks (centre) was a great influence in midfield. The former Millwall and Gillingham man played from 1976 to 1981, making 237 appearances and scoring a dozen goals before moving to Barking. Crowborough-born Tony Sitford (right) first joined the club in 1962 and will always be remembered for scoring the stunning goal at Carlisle in January 1963 that saw Fleet reach the fourth round of the FA Cup for the first time. He left for Dartford in 1963 for a six-year stint before returning to Stonebridge Road. He made 249 appearances in all, scoring 51 goals. The former Brighton man took over from Alf Ackerman in 1974 and became the club's longest-serving manager before being sacked in December 1980.

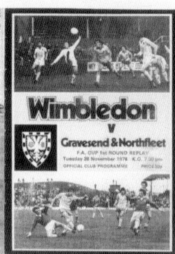

Above: After a long spell with little FA Cup success the club reached the first round proper in 1978/79 and again in 1979/80 losing out unluckily on both occasions to Football League outfits Wimbledon 1-0 in a replay and Torquay by the same scoreline the following year.

Below: Geoff Idle (1950-) was a former Chelsea junior who played for Folkestone and Bexley United before signing for Fleet in 1976. He gave outstanding service as a full-back for six years before a knee injury ended his career in 1982. Geoff made 299 appearances and scored 5 goals during one of the club's most successful periods and had a benefit game against Fulham.

seven

Down, Down and Up 1980-1989

Gravesend reached the first round of the FA Cup for a third year running in 1980/81 and should have progressed against Isthmian League St Albans City at Stonebridge Road. A poor performance allowed the Saints to win via two penalties from their full-back Geoff Whitehead in the no.2 shirt. Brian Gregory (8) and Phil Stonebridge (6), who scored Fleet's last-minute goal, are on the attack.

Chatham Reliance
Building Society
ASSETS EXCEED £50 MILLION
Member of the Building Societies Association

Ashford Town Colours: All Green	Gravesend & Northfleet Colours: Red & White
1 PETER CARMEN	1 COLIN LEWINGTON
2 CLIVE HICKSON	2 GEOFF IDLE
3 PETER McROBERT	3 GEORGE JACKS
4 TIM HOGBEN	4 KEN BURRETT
5 JOHN BARROW	5 JEFF BRYANT
6 GRAHAM JORDAN	6 ALAN HART
7 ADRIAN CARTER	7 BOB DUDMAN
8 KEVIN RAYNOR	8 ~~GARY WILLIAMS~~ DYER
9 JOHN YOUNG	9 CHARLIE POOLEY
10 PETER AMBLER	10 PHIL STONEBRIDGE
11 MICKY JOWETT	11 ~~TREVOR SMITH~~ ALDOUS
Sub: DES PARTINGTON	Sub: ~~GARRY ALDOUS~~ WILLIAMS

Referee: R. J. Clements (Tonbridge)
Linesmen: J. B. Roffey (Ashford) Red flag
M. T. Denman (Bexleyheath) Yellow flag

PRIOR to the game both teams and the officials will be presented to Mr D. J. C. Gilchrist, Director of the Chatham Reliance Building Society and to Mr J. Blackburn, Chairman of the Kent County Football Association. The KCFA/Chatham Reliance Building Society Senior Cup will be presented by Mr Gilchrist.

After a twenty-eight-year, wait the Kent Senior Cup is won in 1981 with a 2-0 victory over Ashford Town at Maidstone with goals from Charlie Pooley and Gary Aldous. Captain Geoff Idle is chaired around the ground by Jeff Bryant and Charlie Pooley.

Left: Liverpool-born former Everton, Bradford City, Swindon, Carlisle and Birmingham central defender Stan Harland (1940-2001). After Southern League experience as player-manager of Yeovil, he was brought to Gravesend in a last throw of the dice to try and avoid relegation from the Alliance League in February 1982, but the ploy failed and he left early in 1982/83 along with chairman Roger Easterby, who had brought him to the club.

Below: The 1983/84 side that exceeded expectations by finishing fourth in the Southern League Premier Division – the club's highest position. From left to right, back row: Fred Wilmshurst (director), Andy Wallace, Trevor Bonneywell (director), John Palfreman (secretary), David Hockley (vice chairman), Gary Aldous, Daryl Lucas (assistant secretary), Tom Jenner (director). Middle row: Gary Julians, Steve Hermitage, Trevor Burke, Ken Burrett, Roger Kent, Kelvin Bright, Geoff Eyers, Alan Risk, Geoff Idle, Mick Ward (physio). Front row: Paul Everest, Steve Brignall, Tony Burns (manager), Ray Tumbridge, Lionel Ball (chairman), Kevin Wallis, Alan Hart.

Right: Tony Burns (1944-), born in Edenbridge, was manager of Gravesend from 1982 to 1985 after a fine career as a goalkeeper with his local club Tonbridge and then Arsenal, Brighton, Charlton, Crystal Palace, Brentford and Plymouth, with a four-year spell in South Africa sandwiched in between. His managerial career also began at Tonbridge and after he left Fleet without having collected any trophies he had a further spell with them.

Above: Ken Burrett, in his last full season at the club, helps himself to a goal at Bromley in the 1983/84 FA Cup steering it past old adversary Dickie Guy in a convincing 4-0 win at Hayes Lane. Ken notched up a record 504 appearances and 26 goals between 1971 and 1984.

Left: Willie O'Sullivan (1959–) was a Lambeth-born midfielder who began at Charlton, for whom he made a single first-team appearance. Willie had a long and successful spell at Dartford before signing for Fleet in 1983. He played 91 games and scored 12 goals for the club before leaving for Fisher in 1985.

Above left: Alan Risk (1964–). Only seventeen when he broke into Fleet's Alliance team as a central defender, Alan played for the club for four seasons, making 128 appearances and scoring a single goal. Always in demand because of his calm, assured displays, he moved to Dagenham in 1985 but injuries blighted his later years.

Above right: As the son of Len Julians, a fine marksman for Arsenal and Millwall, Gary Julians always had a lot to live up to and he certainly proved prolific, even though it was at a lower level. In two spells with Gravesend & Northfleet (1983-1984 and 1988-1990) he scored 36 goals in 123 games.

Right: Paul Burnham holds up the Player of the Year trophy in 1984. Signed from Tonbridge, his goalkeeping in two spells with Fleet (1982-1985 and 1990-1992) was always of a high standard in 168 games.

Colin Dalton played 269 games as a central defender for Fleet from 1983 to 1991 and is seen challenging Welling's prolific marksman Gary Abbott, who himself played a handful of games for Gravesend towards the end of a long career.

Above left: Liverpool-born Alan Whittle (1950-) won a Football League Championship medal with Everton while still in his teens and later played for Crystal Palace and Leyton Orient before finishing his career with a season at Gravesend in 1984/85, making 14 appearances and scoring once.

Above right: Terry Naylor (1948-). Born in Islington, this full-back or central defender played more than 300 times for Tottenham and Charlton between 1969 and 1983 before finishing his senior career at Gravesend in 1984/85 making 47 appearances and scoring once.

A dismal 1985/86 season saw Gravesend relegated from the Southern League Premier Division with only nine wins, one of which came as a result of this Paul Kenny header in a 1-0 victory over Kings Lynn.

Aboive left: Mark Penfold (1956–). This Woolwich-born full-back appeared to have a long Football League career ahead of him until breaking a leg after playing 65 games for Charlton whilst still a teenager. He signed for Fleet from Bromley in 1984, remaining until 1990, making 238 appearances and scoring 7 goals.

Above right: Leroy Bess breezed into the club like a breath of fresh air in 1983 with a string of exciting displays down the wing. He had three different spells up to 1992, making 80 appearances and scoring 18 goals for Gravesend.

The 1986/87 team finished sixth in the Southern League Southern Division. From left to right, back row: David Hockley (chairman), Mark Gregory, Trevor Bonneywell (director), Grant Gallagher, Dean Woodward, Geoff Cook, Mr Holm (sponsor), Dennis Moore, Jon Moore, Geoff Brittain (physio), Colin Dalton, Eddie Presland (manager), Daryl Lucas (secretary). Front row: Wayne Godden, Steve Rutter, Mark Penfold, Mark Freeman.

Mark Penfold curls one straight into the net from a corner against Hastings in the 1986/87 season to put Fleet 2-1 up; they eventually won 3-2.

eight

More Ups
and Downs
1990-1999

Above: Colin Blewden was on target in a 3-1 win over Halesowen in March 1991 but is foiled by the visitors' goalkeeper on this occasion.

Relegation was soon on the cards in the 1991/92 season. Here Neil Grice fires past Ian George to score for Fisher. George was later sent off but Fleet managed a 2-2 draw. However, they were destined for bottom spot.

12 October 1992 and a new destination with a visit to Sussex League Burgess Hill for an FA Cup tie. Lee Graves wins a heading duel as Marcus Smart (4), John Cooper (2), David Flint (8) and Dean Wells (3) look on. A Chris Fordred goal proved decisive for the Fleet.

Opposite below: Tony Stapley foils a Margate attack in a first qualifying round FA Cup tie at Hartsdown Park in September 1990. Although the game finished 2-2, Margate eased to a 4-1 replay win at Stonebridge Road. The white-shorted John Palmer, who made 194 appearances between 1985 and 1990, is the other Fleet player in the picture.

Prolific marksman Steve Portway always had respect from defenders. Here he is closely watched by Fisher defenders shortly before signing for Gloucester City in a £17,500 move in November 1994.

Above left: Simon Ullathorne was a much-travelled winger who joined Gravesend from Croydon in November 1991 but was a native of Cumbria, having previously played for Workington and Cleator Moor Celtic. Simon played a major role in the promotion side of 1993/94. He played 123 games and scored 17 goals for the club before moving to Hastings in 1994.

Above right: Matt Gubbins was another key member of that promotion side with some impressive displays in central defence. Signed from Ashford in November 1992, he played 151 games, scoring twice, and played a key role in the FA Cup run of 1995/96.

Few would have guessed when Godalming were crushed by a record 7-0 scoreline that the road would finally end at Villa Park four months later. Here Mark Munday fires in one of the goals.

Ready for the match of their lives! Players line up before taking on Aston Villa on 6 January 1996. From left to right, back row: Dean Harpley, Dave Walker, John Glover, Lee Turner, Colin Blewden, Mark Munday, Micky Cotter, Chris Weller (manager), Matt Gubbins, Mark Leahy, Mick Ward (physio). Front row: Jimmy Jackson, Paul Wilson, Ian Gibbs, Dave Powell, Grant Best, Clint Gooding, Peter Mortley.

A sizzling shot from Savo Milosevic finally ends Gravesend's brave resistance as Aston Villa win 3-0 in front of 26,000.

Beaten but unbowed after the game.

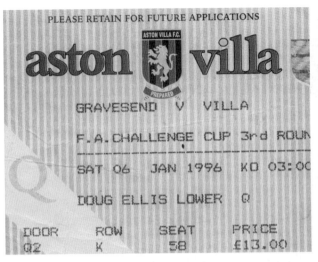

Above and right: The match ticket and programme from a day everyone at Gravesend & Northfleet will remember.

Above: Champions! Fleet players pose in front of delighted supporters after being presented with the Southern League South Division shield in 1994.

Left: Tom Warrilow was the inspirational captain of the 1993/94 promotion side. He had three different spells with the club between 1982 and 1996.

Above: The club's best attacking combination for many years was that of Steve Portway and behind him Mickey Cotter. Together they were the scourge of the opposition in the early 1990s.

Left: Gary Aldous had six different spells as a player with the club between 1980 and 1991 and also had a four-year spell as manager from 1991 to 1995. In 118 appearances for the club he scored 27 goals.

Opposite: Two all-time Fleet heroes: record goalscorer Steve Portway and record appearance maker Ken Burrett, as Ken presents Steve with the Player of the Year trophy.

Left: Two great stalwarts of the club: long-time chairman Lionel Ball and long-time Supporters' Association chairman Mick Baines at the annual cricket match between the club and supporters in 1991.

Below: Lee Turner is under pressure from the Stevenage forwards as Fleet lose out 5-1 in the FA Cup fourth qualifying round of 1996/97. Lee was made the scapegoat, despite having kept more clean sheets than any other goalkeeper, and new manager Steve Lovell allowed him to move to Margate.

Photo by Kent Today.
Back Row Left to Right: Don Turner (Kit Manager), Phil Hariaford
(Reserve Team Manager), Stacey Joseph, Richard Dimmock,
Darren Brodrick, Dean Harpley, Darren Smith, Paul Sansome,
Craig Wilkins, Andy Adebowale, Darren Gowler, Danny Stanton,
Anthony Jones, Andy Ford (Manager), Mick Ward (Physio).
Front Row Left to Right: Glenn Billeness,
Cory Campbell, Jimmy Jackson, Steve Portway,
Dave Powell, Mark Newson, Gary Smith, Justin Skinner,
Paul Wegman, Richard Ponsford, Kirk Doddson.

The club take a photo call before the start of what was to prove a moderate 1998/99 season.

Dave Powell scores twice at Chesham in the 1998/99 season but Fleet still suffer a 3-2 defeat. Signed from Sheppey in 1995, Dave scored 60 goals in 225 games in a five-year stay, the highlight of which was in his first season when he finished top scorer in the FA Cup. He moved to Crawley in 2000.

Craig Wilkins tussles with the Oxford City defence in 1998. Signed from Tonbridge in 1997, he had a six-year stay at Stonebridge Road in which he played 256 games and scored 36 times playing as both a central defender and striker.

Jimmy Bullard aims for goal against Aldershot in August 1998. Signed from Dartford, he soon made an impact with his skill and energy and by February he had moved on to West Ham after just six months with Gravesend for a club record £35,000. He then moved to Peterborough and then to Wigan, where he really made an impact.

Steve Portway and Craig Wilkins in action in a 4-3 defeat at Yeading, in what proved to be Port's last season with the club.

Above and right: One of Gravesend's best wins of the 1990s was the 2-0 victory over Colchester in the FA Cup first round in 1995. Here Mickey Cotter is putting Peter Cawley under pressure.

MISTER HAM MAN

Gravesend & Northfleet F. C. Ltd
Stonebridge Road, Northfleet, Kent DA11 9BA
Telephone: 01474 533796
**PLEASE BE IN THE STADIUM 15 MINUTES
PRIOR TO KICK-OFF**

F.A. CHALLENGE CUP

FIRST ROUND PROPER

SATURDAY 11th NOVEMBER 1995
KICK OFF 3.00 p.m.

GRAVESEND & NORTHFLEET
v
COLCHESTER UNITED

ADULT - GROUND ONLY £7 Inc. VAT

THE FLEET

Player-manager Steve Lovell (10) shows how to do it in his year-long spell in charge (1996/97) in this 2-1 home defeat by Baldock. The former Welsh international had previously played for Crystal Palace, Millwall and Gillingham.

Nick Hegley, seen here firing in a goal against Hendon in 1999, was a pacy forward who had three seasons with Gravesend.

Left: Minehead-born Andy Ford (1954-) began with his home-town team before moving into the Football League with Bournemouth, Swindon, Southend and Gillingham at full-back. Despite having only limited managerial experience, he was appointed Gravesend manager in 1997 and after a rocky start became the club's longest-serving manager (1997-2005) and, perhaps more importantly, the most successful, winning five trophies.

Below: Jimmy Jackson proudly holds his England shirt up after becoming the first player from the Fleet to earn such an honour (playing for England non-League) and in 2005 reached another milestone by breaking Ken Burrett's long-standing appearance record. The Gravesend-born-and-bred player had played for the club since 1994 apart from one season at Dagenham, but remained part-time to help with the family farm just outside of town in Cobham. He left the Fleet in 2006 when the club required that all players be full-time.

Above left: The Ryman Isthmian League title was won at Bedford after a season-long battle with Canvey Island thanks to a 1-0 win with a goal from Che Stadhart.

Above right: Steve Restarick scored twice to bring the Kent Senior Cup back to Gravesend after an eighteen-year wait in a 3-0 win over Folkestone. He began his career at Colchester and played for several other Kent clubs.

Francis Duku was the lynchpin of the Gravesend defence that gained promotion back to the Conference. He joined Fleet in 2000, moving on to Lewes in 2004.

THE KENT COUNTY FOOTBALL ASSOCIATION
KENT SENIOR CUP FINAL
at
Stonebridge Road, Northfleet

1889   2000

FOLKESTONE INVICTA
-v-
GRAVESEND & NORTHFLEET F.C.

MONDAY 1st May 2000
KICK OFF 3.00 p.m.
Souvenir Programme £2.00

Left and below: The programme from the Gravesend *v.* Folkestone Kent Senior Cup final of 2000. Fleet would go on to beat Dover 4-0 in the following season's final and Margate 5-0 in 2002 to complete a spectacular hat-trick of cup successes.

Opposite: The new century provided a good start to the club's FA Cup ambitions with several good performances. The match against Notts County, featuring top scorer Che Stadhart on the cover, had to be moved to Gillingham because of constant waterlogging of the Stonebridge Road pitch.

FOLKESTONE INVICTA	GRAVESEND & NORTHFLEET
Colours: *Black & Amber striped shirts, Black shorts, Amber Socks*	Colours *Red shirts, White shorts, Red socks*

FOLKESTONE INVICTA	GRAVESEND & NORTHFLEET
1. DAVE WIETECHA	1. DARREN SMITH
2. ANDY MORRIS	2. MATT LEE
3. IAN HAYES	3. JIMMY JACKSON
4. ANDY LARKIN	4. DARREN GOWLER
5. LEE PALMER	5. CORY CAMPBELL
6. BILLY MANUEL	6. CRAIG WILKINS
7. CARLTON WYNTER	7. STEVE RESTARICK
8. PAUL CHAMBERS	8. LEE SPILLER
9. STEVE LAWRENCE	9. DAVE POWELL
10. NICKY DENT	10. CHE STADHART
11. JEFF ROSS	11. NICK HEGLEY
12. BRETT SMITH	12. JONATHON DIFFORD
14. JAMES DRYDEN	14. KIRK DODGSON
15. JOHN AYLING	15. DREW WATKINS
Manager: Mr N Cugley	Manager: Mr A Ford

REFEREE   M S Yerby   Assistant Referees F. Mead   J. Wills   Fourth Official   D. Buck
EXTRA TIME - If the scores are level after ninety minutes, then extra time (two 15 minute periods) will be played. If the scores remain level the match will be decided by kicks from the penalty mark

PRESENTATION - The presentation of the Cup and awards will be made by Mr Barry Bright

Gravesend & Northfleet F.C.

est. 1946

v

Notts County

FA Cup 1st Round Proper

Saturday 18th November 2000
Kick Off 3.00pm

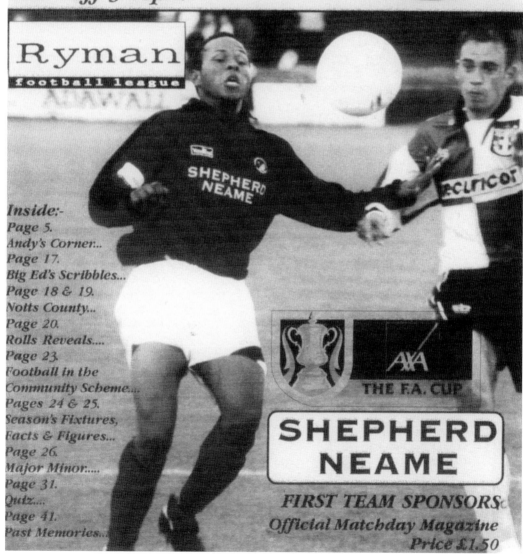

Inside:-
Page 5.
Andy's Corner...
Page 17.
Big Ed's Scribbles...
Page 18 & 19.
Notts County...
Page 20.
Rolls Reveals....
Page 23.
Football in the
Community Scheme....
Pages 24 & 25.
Season's Fixtures,
Facts & Figures...
Page 26.
Major Minor.....
Page 31.
Quiz....
Page 41.
Past Memories...

THE F.A. CUP

SHEPHERD NEAME

FIRST TEAM SPONSORS
Official Matchday Magazine
Price £1.50

Gravesend visited the McAlpine Stadium to take on Huddersfield in the 2001 competition and were desperately unlucky to lose 2-1 to an injury-time goal. Below, Fleet take a sensational second-minute lead when Nathan Clarke heads Elliot Martin's teasing corner into his own net.

A great win at eventual Conference champions Chester was the highlight of the 2003 competition, with Justin Skinner firing in the winner from the penalty spot.

The FLEET

v

NOTTS COUNTY

Saturday 6 December
Kick-off 5.35pm

TheFA
CUP

Princi███ ███ponsor:
GLADWISH
█AND SALES
Associate Spons██rs:

Matchday
Magazine
£2.50

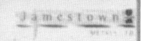

GRAVESEND REPORTER

Above: Charlie Macdonald was comfortably top scorer in the 2005/06 season despite an injury-hit season. He made a handful of Premiership appearances for Charlton in 2001.

Opposite: The win over Chester City in the first round of the FA Cup provided another joust at Notts County in the second round, this time in front of a national live audience on Sky television, but alas the result was a repeat of the 2000 game – a narrow 2-1 win for County.

Ross Smith (born 1980). Canadian-born central defender Smith, signed from Margate in 2005, swept the board at the end-of-season awards for 2005/06.

Born in Hampstead in 1971, Bobby Bowry has played at a high level with Crystal Palace, Millwall and Colchester. He was an influential figure for Gravesend during the 2005/06 season.

Justin Skinner (born 1972) was signed from Aylesbury, previously having played in the top division of English football with Wimbledon. He left after a season but returned in in 2001, making 180 appearances and scoring 8 goals from left-back before leaving for Margate in 2006.

Danny Slatter, formerly of Chelsea, is a major hope for the future at Stonebridge Road.

Left: Liam Daish (1968–) became the club's twenty-seventh manager in February 2005. Portsmouth-born, he had earned a reputation as a strong, no-nonsense defender with Portsmouth, Cambridge United, Birmingham and Coventry before injury brought an end to his playing career while he was still in his late twenties.

Below: Charlie Macdonald might be on his knees but he has just scored the only goal of the game to see off high riders Morecambe in 2005.

Above and below: Following the shock departure of Andy Ford, a benefit game was arranged between the 2001/02 side that had been champions of the Ryman League and the 2004/05 side.

Above: Hopes for the future. The club now have their own training facility at the former Beauwater Sports Club. Excellent sports and social facilities and an ever-increasing local population offer great future potential for Gravesend & Northfleet Football Club.

Left: Steve McKimm joined Gravesend in 2001 from Kingstonian and provided the drive and experience that were so important on the rise to the Conference. Illness and injury reduced his influence but he fought back to regain his place in 2006.

Above left: Lee Protheroe, a defender who first came to Gravesend on loan from Canvey Island in 2003/04 before making the deal permanent the following season.

Above right: Highly rated midfielder Andy Drury, who completed three good seasons before leaving for Lewes at the end of the 2005/6 season.

Right: Jay Saunders accepts a Player of the Month award from manager Liam Daish in 2005. Jay began as a youth team player with the club but moved to Margate, before returning in 2005. Influential in midfield, he also has the knack of scoring important goals.

Other titles published by Stadia

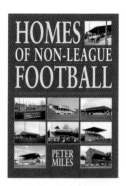

Homes of Non-League Football
PETER MILES

The people's game touches many levels, and with ninety per cent of all football matches being played outside the hallowed halls of the Premiership and Football League, non-League football forms a vital part of our nation's sporting heritage. This book catalogues, in words and pictures, the 350 biggest, best-loved, most historically important and beautiful non-League grounds.

0 7524 2723 7

Kent CCC 100 Greats
DAVID ROBERTSON, HOWARD MILTON & DEREK CARLAW

In its long history the county of Kent has had more than its fair share of great cricketers. Men like Nicholas Felix in the mid-nineteenth century led the way, and the likes of Frank Woolley and Colin Blythe followed. This book features illustrations, career statistics and biographies of 100 of the finest, including cricketers from 'The Glory Years' of the 1960s and '70s, such as Colin Cowdrey and Derek Underwood, and some of Kent's best-loved players of the last few years, including Mark Ealham and Matthew Fleming.

0 7524 3454 3

Kent CCC Classic Matches
DAVID ROBERTSON, HOWARD MILTON & DEREK CARLAW

Kent CCC has a long and proud tradition stretching back over 150 years. The club has been witness to some classic encounters over this time and here three long-term followers of Kent look back at fifty of the finest of them. With the earliest match dating back to 1839, this book provides a fascinating glimpse of some of the finest moments in the club's long history, while the inclusion of games from 2004 and 2005 will provide memories that even Kent's youngest supporters can enjoy reliving.

0 7524 3785 2

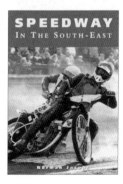

Speedway in the South-East
NORMAN JACOBS

From speedway's introduction to Great Britain in 1928 up to the present day, the south-east of England has been one of the main centres of the sport, boasting leading teams like Eastbourne, Rye House and Arena Essex. This book covers the history of those tracks as well as many others that have, in their day, provided thrills and excitement to the many thousands of speedway supporters in the area around London.

0 7524 2725 3

If you are interested in purchasing other books published by Stadia, or in case you have difficulty finding any Tempus books in your local bookshop, you can also place orders directly through our website

www.tempus-publishing.com